Strategize! 3e

Experiential Exercises in Strategic Management

Strategize! 3e

Experiential Exercises in Strategic Management

C. Gopinath
Suffolk University

Julie Siciliano
Western New England College

SOUTH-WESTERN
CENGAGE Learning

Australia • Brazil • Japan • Korea • Mexico • Singapore • Spain • United Kingdom • United States

Strategize! Experiential Exercises in Strategic Management, Third Edition
C. Gopinath & Julie Siciliano

Vice President of Editorial, Business:
Jack W. Calhoun

Vice President/Editor-in-Chief: Melissa Acuna

Acquisitions Editor: Michele Rhoades

Developmental Editor: Ruth Belanger

Marketing Director/Manager: Nathan Anderson

Marketing Coordinator: Suellen Ruttkay

Content Project Manager: Abigail Greshik

Production Manager: Jennifer Ziegler

Media Editor: Danny Bolan

Manufacturing Buyer: Doug Wilke

Production Service: Pre-PressPMG

Copyeditor: Pre-Press PMG

Compositor: Pre-Press PMG

Senior Art Director: Tippy McIntosh

Cover/Internal Design: Red Hangar Design LLC

Cover Image: © Getty Images/Gregor Schuster.

Permissions Acquisitions Manager/Image:
Deanna Ettinger

Permissions Acquisitions Manager/Text:
Roberta Broyer

For product information and technology assistance, contact us at
Cengage Learning Customer & Sales Support, 1-800-354-9706

For permission to use material from this text or product,
submit all requests online at **cengage.com/permissions**
Further permissions questions can be emailed to
permissionrequest@cengage.com

Library of Congress Control Number: 2008943513

ISBN-13: 978-0-324-59713-4

ISBN-10: 0-324-59713-4

Package ISBN-13: 978-0-324-59638-0

Package ISBN-10: 0-324-59638-3

South-Western Cengage Learning
5191 Natorp Boulevard
Mason, OH 45040
USA

Cengage Learning products are represented in Canada by Nelson Education, Ltd.

For your course and learning solutions, visit **academic.cengage.com**

Purchase any of our products at your local college store or at our preferred online store **www.ichapters.com**

Printed in the United States of America
1 2 3 4 5 6 7 8 12 11 10 09

BRIEF CONTENTS

PART I   **UNDERSTANDING STRATEGIC MANAGEMENT** 1

PART II   **DESIGNING STRATEGY** 35

PART III   **IMPLEMENTING STRATEGY** 99

PART IV   **INDUSTRY ANALYIS** 133

PART V   **SEMESTER PROJECTS** 159

CONTENTS

PART I UNDERSTANDING STRATEGIC MANAGEMENT

Strategy Session 1 Decision Making at the Strategic and Operational Level 3
Exercise: Innkeepers of America 5

Strategy Session 2 Understanding the Concept of Strategy 7
Exercise: How Do You Define Strategy? 9

Strategy Session 3 Communicating Purpose Through Mission Statements 11
*Exercise 1: How Well Do These Organizations Communicate
Their Purpose? 14*
Exercise 2: Video—Create a Mission Statement for Caribou Coffee 18
Exercise 3: Video—Create a Mission Statement for Fossil, Inc. 19

Strategy Session 4 The Board's Role in Corporate Governance 21
Exercise: Translating the Board's Role into Guidelines for Practice 23

Strategy Session 5 Viewing Strategy from the Stakeholder Perspective 24
Exercise: 1: Wal-Mart and Banking 30
Exercise 2: Role Playing Global Chemical Stakeholders' Interests and Power 32

PART II DESIGNING STRATEGY

Strategy Session 6 Forces Affecting Competitive Strategy 37
Exercise: Intensity of Competition in the Casino Gambling Industry 39

Strategy Session 7 Generating a Plan of Action: SWOT (TOWS) Analysis 47
Exercise 1: An Action Plan for Robin Hood 49
Exercise 2: Video—Kropf Fruit Company—Future Strategy 53

Strategy Session 8 Developing Generic Strategy 55
Exercise 1: Choosing How to Compete in the Lodging Industry 57
Exercise 2: Video—The Generic Strategy of Fossil, Inc. 60

Strategy Session 9 Building Competitive Advantage 61
Exercise: Build Your Intended Strategy 63

Strategy Session 10 Viewing Corporate Strategy from the Core Competencies Perspective 85
Exercise: Corporate Strategy at Honda 67

Strategy Session 11 Global Strategic Alliances 71
Exercise: Renewing the General Motors–Toyota Alliance 73

Strategy Session 12 Identifying Transnational Strategies 79
Exercise: Global Operations of Bata Shoe and Nike 81

Strategy Session 13   Understanding Turnaround Management 87
                          Exercise: The Decline–Turnaround Sequence   89

Strategy Session 14   Scenario Planning: Innovative Approaches for the Future 93
                          Exercise: Develop Some Scenarios   95

PART III   IMPLEMENTING STRATEGY

Strategy Session 15   Succeeding in Strategy Formulation and Implementation 101
                          Exercise: Diagnosing Problems at Hewlett-Packard   103

Strategy Session 16   Structuring to Support Strategy 107
                          Exercise: Designing Organizational Structures for Club Ed   110

Strategy Session 17   Strategy Implementation Using the 7-S Model 115
                          Exercise: Transition at PeopleSoft   117

Strategy Session 18   Corporate Sustainability 123
                          Exercise: Video—BP's Level of Corporate Sustainability   126

Strategy Session 19   Monitoring Strategy Implementation Through the Balanced Scorecard *129*
                          *Exercise: Everyone Knows the Score When a Major League Baseball Team Ties Performance
                          to Its Mission   131*

PART IV   INDUSTRY ANALYIS

Lodging Industry Profile 135

Template for Industry Survey 139

Assessing Strategic Performance Through Financial Analysis 141

Case Study 1   Strategic Alternatives at Mercury Telecom 143

Case Study 2   Caffeine Satisfaction: Rivalry Among the Coffee Shops 149

PART V   SEMESTER PROJECTS

Team Projects A and B 161
                          Project A: Comparing Two Organizations in the Same Industry   161
                          Project B: Identifying Strategic Issues at Local Business Organizations   162

MICA Method of Case Analysis and Discussion 163

References and Sources 169

Index 171

INTRODUCTION

The strategic management/business policy course is among the most challenging in the business curriculum—and for good reason. It is designed to teach the skills of strategic thinking and analysis, and it requires that students integrate information from courses throughout the business curriculum. The goal of the course is equally challenging: to learn strategic management theories and concepts in order to "do" strategy.

Cases have been an important and traditional component of the strategic management course. Indeed, cases are excellent devices for compelling students to appreciate the intricacies of making decisions within a context. However, what is often missing in case-driven courses is that critical bridge between understanding strategic models and applying them in ways that ensure active engagement with case material at levels beyond the merely factual. Computer-based strategy simulations, likewise, give students lots of practice in making decisions, but they are also somewhat limiting as students rarely get to experiment with appropriate models or concepts before attempting to apply them to simulation specifics. *Strategize!* bridges this gap by providing a series of "Strategy Sessions," through which students can evaluate theories in incremental and structured ways in advance of applying them to resolve strategic business problems.

These 19 unique action-oriented Strategy Sessions present experiential exercises and projects for use in class and out: as breaks away from straight lectures, as segues to case discussions, as homework, as collaborative assignments, as lecture launchers, as pre-class case preparation, and as similar alternatives. Exercises can be drawn on when theories are first introduced and discussed in class or at other times during the semester to reinforce previously reviewed material.

Each Strategy Session makes a complete turn through the active learning cycle of thought, action, feedback, and assessment. In our view, working productively, staying motivated, and actively exploring potentially relevant theories generate a greater probability of successfully achieving the goals of demanding capstone courses, such as strategic management, and so we have incorporated these aims into our exercises. Figure I.1 depicts the experiential learning cycle as we implement it.

Our approach to experiential learning, as Figure I.1 shows, incorporates successive rounds of reflection, experimentation, and assessment. Our exercises focus on building abilities to apply appropriate strategic theories and models to reach meaningful conclusions, along the way strengthening critical thinking skills, analytical skills, and the ability to make defensible decisions and generate persuasive arguments.

Testing the strengths and limitations of theories and getting regular feedback about one's understanding of them form an important complement to the case-study method. The design of each Strategy Session brings together a number of elements that support the thinking/acting/assessing components of the active learning cycle:

1. Brief explanations—or readings—of relevant concepts, wherein the academic purpose of the exercise is made absolutely clear.

2. Structured applications.

FIGURE I.1 EXPERIENTIAL LEARNING CYCLE

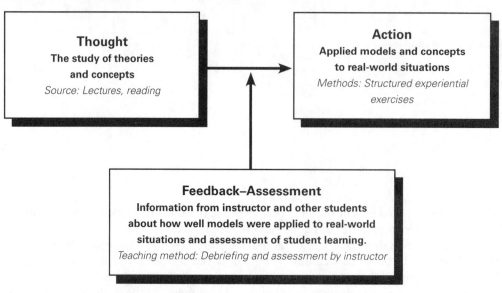

3. Instructor-facilitated debriefings.

4. Assessments of individual participation and accountability.

5. Assessments of overall learning.

Some Strategy Sessions require teams, whereas others may be completed on an individual or team basis, depending on instructor preference. To promote individual accountability, many sessions have assessment forms to document the student's understanding of the work before performing an activity. All sessions have assessments to be administered after each exercise. The forms vary and either gauge how well students fit strategic concepts and tools to given problems or provide feedback to the instructor about the class session in general. (Assessment literature suggests that the formats vary from one session to another.)

As in any course that revolves around experiential methods, the instructor plays a crucial role acting as moderator, questioner, and lecturer, probing for details, for support for arguments, and for alternative courses of action. *Strategize!,* through the simultaneous publication of a resource manual for instructors, can provide useful strategies for managing exercises in the classroom. More information about instructor support materials is available at **http://www.cengage.com/management/Gopinath**—but a quick reference of Figure I.2, the Strategy Session Matrix, shows how each Strategy Session complements chapter discussions in several leading strategic management texts. Detailed guidelines for debriefing, providing feedback, and assessing student learning, are provided in the aforementioned instructor's manual (0324596413).

Organization of the Book

In this third edition, we have added a new exercise on building competitive advantage, a new exercise on corporate sustainability, a new case about Mercury Telecom, new companies for the exercises (such as Wal-Mart, Honda, Hewlett-Packard, and BP), and a new template for financial analysis. We have also revised and updated the information in Strategy Sessions and exercises retained from the second edition.

Strategize! is divided into five parts. Parts I, II, and III, on understanding strategic management, designing strategy, and implementing strategy, set up a series of Strategy Sessions designed primarily for in-class use. The sequencing of Strategy Sessions is key because it simulates the steps in the strategic management process common to most textbooks in the field. Strategy Sessions are intended to provide students with an active experience of concepts. Each session opens with a precisely stated learning objective, followed by a short reading that frames the theory or concept that is highlighted in the real drama: the session's featured exercise. As noted earlier, exercises have been developed for students to complete individually or in groups. However, we have also designed them to increase variety and interest in the classroom.

Part IV features a profile of the lodging industry. Industry data is culled from secondary sources readily available to decision makers in the real world. This profile is used principally as background information for certain Strategy Sessions, but it also serves as an example of the industry overview that students should build for assigned cases or projects. A template for students to use in gathering information on an industry, as a precursor for other kinds of in-depth analysis, is also included in this part as is the template for students to use in undertaking analysis of financial statements. Two cases follow describing a telecom company in a crisis situation ripe for a turnaround and the rivalry in coffee beverage retailing.

Part V consists of two optional, semester-long projects, along with a framework (the MICA method) for in-class discussion of strategic management cases—a format that facilitates full-class participation. The projects require field research and decision making by students in teams. The MICA method is an alternative to the standard Socratic approach to case discussion and is designed to generate maximum participation by students in class using a structured format. It also incorporates a technique for clarifying grading criteria.

Acknowledgments

We would like to record our sincere appreciation to South-Western/Cengage Learning for its continued support of our efforts in propagating experiential learning as a means to understanding strategic management. In particular, our thanks go to Michele Rhoades, Senior Acquisitions Editor, and Ruth Belanger, Senior Editorial Assistant, for their extensive help on this third edition.

We wish to thank the following users of the book for their comments and suggestions in the production of this third edition:

Bindu Arya
University of Missouri-St. Louis

Tom Aylward
Suffolk University

James Cordeiro
State University of New York, Brockport

Steve Courter
University of Texas at Austin

Sushil Bhatia
Suffolk University

Bella Butler
Curtin University, Australia

Kalyan Chakravarthy
California State University, Northridge

Lawrence Loh
National University of Singapore

Shalei Simms
Rutgers University

We continue to acknowledge our reviewers for the second edition of *Strategize!*:

Macgorine A. Cassell
Fairmont State College

James J. Cordeiro
State University of New York, Brockport

Sr. Mary M. Fanning
College of Notre Dame

Santo D. Marabella
Moravian College

Bernard Skown
Stevens Institute of Technology

Finally, the exercises and projects described here have benefited from the feedback that we have received over several semesters from our students. We are grateful for their guidance in helping us strike the right chords. Nevertheless, there is always room for further improvement. We welcome your comments, as they will most definitely help us make *Strategize!* even better for you in the future. Please e-mail your experiences or register your comments at **http://www.cengage.com/management/Gopinath.**

C. Gopinath   Julie Siciliano
Suffolk University   *Western New England College*
cgopinat@suffolk.edu   jsicilia@wnec.edu

Strategy Session Matrix for Strategic Mangement Textbooks

The Strategy Sessions are experiential activities designed to give students practice in applying models and concepts from the strategic management course. These exercises can be included when theories are being discussed in class or at other times during the semester to reinforce previously reviewed material. The correlations grid in Figure I.2 on the facing page shows how the Sessions complement chapter discussions in several leading strategic management texts.

FIGURE I.2   STRATEGY SESSION MATRIX FOR SELECTED STRATEGIC MANAGEMENT TEXTS

Strategy Session	David 11th ed. 2007	Hill & Jones 8th ed. 2008	Hitt, et al. 8th ed. 2009	Wheelen & Hunger 10th ed. 2006	Harrison & St. John 4th ed. 2008	Thompson Strickland & Gamble 15th ed. 2007	Grant 6th ed. 2008	Carpenter & Sanders 2nd ed. 2009	Dess, Lumpkin & Eisner 3rd ed. 2007
1. Decision Making at the Strategic and Operational Level	Ch. 1	Ch. 1	Ch. 1	Ch. 1	Ch. 1	Ch. 1	Ch. 1	Ch. 1	Ch. 1
2. Understanding the Concept of Strategy	Ch. 1	Ch. 1	Ch. 1	Ch. 1	Ch. 1	Ch. 1, 2	Ch. 1,2	Ch. 1	Ch. 1
3. Communicating Purpose Through Mission Statements	Ch. 2	Ch. 1	Ch. 1	Ch. 1	Ch. 4	Ch. 2	Ch. 1	Ch. 2	Ch. 1
4. The Board's Role in Corporate Governance	Ch. 6	Ch. 11	Ch. 10	Ch. 2	Ch. 3	Ch. 2	Ch. 6, 16	Ch. 13	Ch. 1,9
5. Viewing Strategy from the Stakeholder Perspective	Ch. 2	Ch. 11	Ch. 1	Ch. 3	Ch. 1	Ch. 2, 10	Ch. 2	Ch. 2	Ch. 1
6. Forces Affecting Competitive Strategy	Ch. 3	Ch. 2	Ch. 2	Ch. 4	Ch. 2	Ch. 3	Ch. 3, 4	Ch. 4	Ch. 2
7. Generating a Plan of Action: SWOT Analysis	Ch. 6	Ch. 1	Ch. 2, 3	Ch. 6	Ch. 1	Ch. 4	Ch. 1	Ch. 3	Ch. 2
8. Developing Generic Strategy	Ch. 5	Ch. 5	Ch. 4	Ch. 6	Ch. 5	Ch. 5	Ch. 7, 8, 9	Ch. 5	Ch. 5
9. Building competitive strategy	Ch. 5	Ch. 4, 5	Ch. 4, 5	Ch. 6	Ch. 5	Ch. 5	Ch. 7, 8, 9	Ch. 5	Ch. 3, 4, 5
10. Viewing Corporate Strategy from the Core Competencies Perspective	Ch. 5, 6	Ch. 9, 10	Ch. 3, 6, 7	Ch. 7	Ch. 3,6	Ch. 9, 11	Ch. 13, 15, 16	Ch. 7	Ch. 6
11. Global Strategic Alliances	Ch. 1, 5	Ch. 8	Ch. 8, 9	Ch. 7	Ch. 6	Ch. 7, 9	Ch. 4, 13, 15	Ch. 8, 9	Ch. 7
12. Identifying Transnational Strategies	Ch.1, 5	Ch. 8	Ch. 8	Ch. 7	Ch. 5	Ch. 7	Ch. 14	Ch. 8	Ch. 7
13. Understanding Turnaround Management	Ch. 5	Ch. 6	Ch. 7	Ch. 7	Ch. 8	Ch. 8	Ch. 12	Ch. 12	Ch. 5
14. Scenario Planning: Innovative Approaches for the Future	Ch. 6	Ch. 1	Ch. 2	Ch. 4	Ch. 2, 4	Ch. 3	Ch. 10	Ch. 4	Ch. 2
15. Succeeding in Strategy Formulation and Implementation	Ch. 7, 8	Ch. 6, 12	Ch. 11, 12	Ch. 9, 10	Ch. 5, 6, 7	Ch. 11, 12, 13	Ch. 7, 16	Ch. 6, 11	Ch. 5, 9, 10
16. Structuring to Support Strategy	Ch. 7	Ch. 12	Ch. 11	Ch. 9	Ch. 7	Ch. 11	Ch. 6	Ch. 11	Ch. 10
17. Strategy Implementation Using the 7-S Model	Ch. 7, 8, 9	Ch. 12, 13	Ch. 11, 12	Ch. 9, 10, 11	Ch. 5, 6, 7	Ch. 11, 12, 13	Ch. 7, 16	Ch. 6, 11	Ch. 9, 10, 11
18. Corporate Sustainability	Ch. 1	Ch. 11	Ch. 1, 12	Ch. 3	Ch. 1	Ch. 10	17	Ch. 2	Ch. 1
19. Monitoring Implementation Through the Balanced Scorecard	Ch. 5, 9	Ch. 11	Ch. 12	Ch. 11	Ch. 8	Ch. 2	Ch. 2	Ch. 11	Ch. 3

Strategize! 3e

Experiential Exercises in Strategic Management

Strategy Session 1

Decision Making at the Strategic and Operational Level   3

Exercise: Innkeepers of America   5

Strategy Session 2

Understanding the Concept of Strategy   7

Exercise: How Do You Define Strategy?   9

Strategy Session 3

Communicating Purpose Through Mission Statements   11

Exercise 1: How Well Do These Organizations Communicate Their Purpose?   14

Exercise 2: Video—Create a Mission Statement for Caribou Coffee   18

Exercise 3: Video—Create a Mission Statement for Fossil, Inc.   19

Strategy Session 4

The Board's Role in Corporate Governance   21

Exercise: Translating the Board's Role into Guidelines for Practice   23

Strategy Session 5

Viewing Strategy from the Stakeholder Perspective   29

Exercise 1: Wal-Mart and Banking   30

Exercise 2: Role Playing Global Chemical Stakeholders' Interests and Power   32

PART I

Understanding Strategic Management

Strategy Session 1

Decision Making at the Strategic and Operational Level

OBJECTIVE

In this session, the concept of strategy is explored by distinguishing it from operational issues. After finishing this reading and performing the accompanying exercise, you will be able to identify strategic and operational-level decisions.

Decisions are constantly made in organizations, and they can broadly be considered to fall in one of two categories. One set of decisions involves the development of strategies for the total organization. These strategic-level decisions include defining the mission and overall corporate goals, determining what businesses to be in, and how to compete in those businesses. The second set of decisions helps to make strategic-level decisions work. They keep the business running efficiently by translating strategies into action in the areas of human resources, finance and accounting, marketing, research and development, and manufacturing. When managers of these business functions choose courses of action, they take their cues from the strategies developed for the total organization. Thus, because strategic decisions affect the firm as a whole and involve creating competitive advantage, it is important to have a clear understanding of the distinction between strategic and operational decision making—however, it is a distinction that is not always easy to make.

> Managers must clearly distinguish operational effectiveness from strategy. Both are essential, but the two agendas are different.
>
> —*Michael E. Porter*

At the start of this strategic management course, the typical way that many view the issues will be from an operational perspective. This is a familiar perspective for business majors with courses of study specializing in one function of the business (e.g., marketing, accounting, computer information systems, etc.). Moreover, individuals with professional experience often make decisions dealing with their particular area of expertise at the operational level. This is not surprising, since up to this point in most curricula, courses are designed around the business functions and provide theory and training at the operational level. In addition, those individuals with professional experience have tended to be members of a single department focused on a business function. Although more and more organizations encourage employees at all levels to view their areas from a broader and strategic perspective, many have not had the opportunity or training to practice strategic thinking. Even when the conceptual distinction between strategic- and operational-level decision making becomes clear, in reality the line separating the two types of decisions is not always obvious. For example, on the face of it, buying a small machine should be considered operational, should it not? But if new equipment is purchased in support of a new *strategic* direction for the firm, is the decision to purchase suddenly strategic in scope? What about an aggregated series of operational decisions, such as purchasing several machines in the production area? If equipment purchases can, in fact, give an organization additional competencies and thereby alter the strategy of the firm, then the answer, perhaps, is yes.

To help clarify what should be viewed as strategic decision making, the following points provide a basis for thinking about issues and decisions from a strategic perspective:

1. Is the decision about changing the firm's position within the industry?
2. Will the decision involve a new business area?
3. Does the decision have a significant financial impact on the firm?
4. Would it evoke a significant response in the environment—that is, from competitors or other stakeholders?

The benefit of distinguishing between the two levels of decision making in the strategic management course is that one begins to develop a type of *strategic thought process*. This helps the strategic manager to recommend decisions that affect the firm as a whole and to better understand the importance of competitive advantage. While effectiveness at both the operational and strategic levels is essential to competitiveness, a focus on operational decisions can result in an organization doing things better than its competitors. However, improvements in operational performance are often easily imitated.

The strategic-level decisions that focus on doing things *differently* are what provide a sustained competitive advantage where an organization preserves meaningful differences with rivals. By the time this strategic management course is completed, how these strategic-level decisions differ from those involving operational-level issues will not only be understood, it will be appreciated, too, in a completely new way.

Exercise

Innkeepers of America

INSTRUCTIONS

After reading the case below, read the statements that follow it and put an S next to the decisions that are strategic and an O next to the ones that are operational.

Innkeepers of America, a medium-sized national hotel chain, has operated successfully for many years in the economy segment of the lodging industry. Its chain of hotels provides rooms that are comfortable and roomy. To keep costs low, the company locates its properties near a major restaurant instead of providing that service itself. The rooms and lobby areas are comfortable with normal accommodations, but extra frills are avoided. Although the company has its own staff of security guards, cleaning and landscaping services are contracted out to local companies.

During the past three years, several new competitors have entered the economy segment of the industry using aggressive pricing strategies. To meet the new competitive threat, management responded with a series of steps over the past two years. They lowered the price of the hotel rooms by 10% last year and again this year with the goal of matching competitor prices. They also created a new advertising campaign that targeted budget-conscious customers by giving them discount coupons for weekend stays. This promotion increased occupancy on the weekends, and plans are to continue it this year. Three new positions were created and filled in the customer service department. Employees were given shares of the company stock as part of a bonus plan. A continental breakfast menu was created. Guests could get bread rolls and breakfast drinks in the lobby or they could get them delivered to their room for an extra fee. Over 50% of the guests used this service. The reservation system was fully computerized, and front-desk employees received four half-day training sessions on the new system. However, despite these changes, the company's overall market share did not increase, and in the last quarter it dropped slightly. The company's net profit margin also declined from the previous year.

Management was concerned, and a meeting was held to review and recommend courses of action. The head of marketing proposed a new company Web site where customers could book reservations online. The operations vice president noted that with the additional customer service staff and features, such as the continental breakfast, the company's image was beginning to change. She recommended that all of the new hotels planned for construction next year be designed with more features to appeal to an upscale market segment. The marketing vice president agreed and noted that an upscale property would allow management to charge higher prices for the rooms to cover the higher costs associated with the upcoming campaigns. The president shared a letter with the group where a major competitor, Economy Lodge, Inc., wanted to merge with Innkeepers of America. According to the president, "This merger would increase our market share by a sizable amount, and we would be able to compete more strongly in the economy segment of this industry. However, before we decide on this and other actions you've recommended, we should rewrite our mission statement so that we have a sense of our core purpose and which decisions we should make to achieve that purpose."

_____ 1. Innkeepers of America's position in the economy segment of the lodging industry.

_____ 2. Locating properties next to a restaurant rather than having food and beverage in-house.

_____ 3. Price of rooms lowered further to meet competition.

_____ 4. New advertising campaign with discount coupons for weekend stays.

_____ 5. Three new customer service positions.

_____ 6. Shares of company stock issued for employee bonuses.

_____ 7. Providing continental breakfast in the lobby.

_____ 8. Room service (for continental breakfast only).

_____ 9. Computerized reservation system.

_____ 10. Training program for front-desk employees.

_____ 11. Web site where reservations can be booked online.

_____ 12. New hotel properties built with additional features to appeal to an upscale market.

_____ 13. Merger with Economy Lodge, Inc.

_____ 14. Rewrite mission statement.

_____ 15. Contracting cleaning and landscaping services.

Strategy Session 2
Understanding the Concept of Strategy

OBJECTIVE

This session's reading and exercise provide the opportunity to explore strategy from several points of view. Knowing multiple definitions helps in understanding the different facets of the concept.

Strategy is a term used in many ways. The exercise in Strategy Session 1 revealed that strategy can be large decisions that managers make. But even smaller, tactical moves can prove to be strategic in certain cases. Early definitions of strategy were the plans that "matched" the organization to its environment, whereas today the formal definitions describe it as a set of decisions and actions that managers take to achieve organizational goals related to achieving strategic competitiveness and earning above-average returns. In addition, the word *strategic* modifies many other words and actions to give them a sense of importance. For example, we read about a "strategic move" or a major "strategic undertaking." Quite often, the debate on what to do and how it is done occurs because of the different meanings attributed to *strategy.* Henry Mintzberg provides five definitions—the "Five P's":

> The field of strategic management cannot afford to rely on a single definition of strategy, indeed the word has long been used implicitly in different ways even if it has traditionally been defined formally in only one.
>
> —Henry Mintzberg

1. **Strategy as a plan.** This is a consciously intended course of action. It could take the form of a set of guidelines or a written report that managers use to guide their decisions. Start-ups usually write a business plan for their future. Some organizations go through a formal planning process and arrive at a document that will guide their actions in the years to come.

2. **Strategy as a pattern.** This is an after-the-fact view of strategy. When we look at organizations over time, as journalists in the business press often do in their reports, we see a "pattern in a stream of actions." We may see a consistency that suggests a direction. When that pattern, which is a "realized" strategy, was not originally intended, it is called "emergent."

3. **Strategy as a position.** Managers see their firm as occupying a space within an environment. This is its position in the market and is often defined in terms of market share. Automotive companies see the market as comprised of several segments, such as minivans, trucks, etc., and set targets in terms of a share of the market.

4. **Strategy as a perspective.** This represents how the organization sees itself, and expresses its way of doing things. It is the organization's way of perceiving the world. 3M declares itself to be a "diversified technology company" and sees new technology as a way of exploiting new markets.

5. **Strategy as a ploy.** This is a short-term tactic or a maneuver that is intended to outwit or preempt competitive strategic moves. For example, a firm that anticipates market growth might announce a five- or ten-fold increase in production capacity. This extensive capacity discourages potential rivals from trying to set up their own

facilities. Another example is if a software company announced a new product that was going to reach the market in a year or so with the result that customers avoid competitive products as they wait for the new software. Another ploy occurs when a company learns about a new innovative product and then slows the introduction by questioning whether the advertising is false or misleading and holding up the introduction process until legal questions are resolved. These examples illustrate how strategic ploys can take the steam out of new offerings.

The different definitions enrich our understanding of how strategies are formed and how the process can be managed. They are also different ways of getting a handle on the term "strategy." As a plan, strategy provides information about what was intended. As a ploy, the focus is on direct competition and how maneuvers can gain advantage for a firm. As a pattern, strategy looks at actions and behaviors, where intentions may have to adjust to a changing environment, revealing the unintended or emergent strategies that often occur. As a position, the focus is on the competitive environment and how organizations struggle for advantage. As a perspective, strategy looks at how a collective group of individuals share values and behave in such a way that they cooperate in the production of specific goods and services.

These definitions enable us to view strategy not only from the important competitive perspective but also to better understand how organizational members help to shape the process. In some ways the definitions may compete by substituting for each other, but they also complement each other. Thus, they are not mutually exclusive. As a diagnostic tool, if we find contradictions in the different P's when applied to an organization, it may suggest confusion in the organization's sense of direction and how it is trying to achieve its goals.

Exercise

How Do You Define Strategy?

INSTRUCTIONS
Reconsider the Innkeepers of America case on page 5. Read it again if necessary. Do you find evidence of the different forms of strategy in the case? Look for statements/phrases in the case that illustrate the different definitions of strategy.

Form of Strategy	Statements/Phrases in Case
Plan	
Pattern	
Position	

(*Continued on next page*)

Form of Strategy	Statements/Phrases in Case
Perspective	
Ploy	

Strategy Session 3
Communicating Purpose Through Mission Statements

OBJECTIVE

This session shows whether organizations define their core purpose by simply describing current product lines and the service they provide—or whether they define their core purpose in terms of the customer needs being satisfied. After finishing this reading, perform the exercises and team activities that follow.

The first responsibility of management is to provide a clear sense of direction for decision making and to guide strategy development. In strategic management, an organization's general and enduring sense of direction is defined as its *mission*. The most common way that organizations attempt to communicate their sense of purpose or direction is through a mission statement.

> Only a clear definition of the mission and purpose of the business makes possible clear and realistic business objectives. It is the foundation for priorities, strategies, plans, and work assignments.
>
> —*Peter F. Drucker*

Overview of Mission Statement Criteria

Mission statements vary considerably in their design. Two basic criteria, however, define for employees, customers, and all stakeholders the organization's highest and most enduring goals:

1. A statement that defines the organization's core purpose in terms of customer needs.

2. A statement that indicates the key beliefs, values, and priorities that managers are committed to and that influence the decisions they make.

Definition of the Organization's Core Purpose

When an organization defines its core purpose, it should make clear the importance people attach to the organization's work. In other words, the organization must define its reason for being.

The mission statement should clearly answer the questions: "What business are we in?" and "What business should we be in?" It is important that these questions be answered in terms of customer needs and not based on the products or services the company currently offers. Some companies make the mistake of simply describing their current product lines or customer segments as their core purpose, when instead they should focus on the customer needs that the business seeks to satisfy. To get at a customer-oriented definition, one method is to answer the question *Why?* several times.

A technique for moving from a product or service orientation to a customer-needs definition of an organization's purpose is shown in Table 1.1, with examples using a company that manufacturers cosmetics and a company that provides market research data, respectively.

TABLE 1.1   MISSION STATEMENTS: MOVING FROM A PRODUCT/SERVICE ORIENTATION TO A CUSTOMER-NEEDS ORIENTATION

Product/Service Definition	Examples
Instruction: Start with a descriptive statement: "We make x products or we provide x services."	Company that manufactures and markets face makeup: *We make quality cosmetics.*
	Company that provides market research to other organizations: *We do research about market characteristics and market demand for companies in a variety of industries.*

Customer-Needs Definition	Examples
Instruction: Answer the question *why* as many times as it takes to get to the fundamental purpose of the organization—or the customer-needs definition. That is, why do we make these products or deliver these services? What needs do the products/ services satisfy?	**Face Makeup Company** ("We make quality cosmetics.") Why? – *We enhance beauty and enable our customers to maintain a youthful appearance.*
	Market Research Organization ("We do research about market characteristics …") Why? – *To provide the best data available so that the customers will understand their markets better.* Why? – *To contribute to our customers' success by helping them understand their markets.*

For many people in a company, it is difficult to think about the organization's purpose in any way other than the product manufactured or the service provided. After all, it is "what we do." Because it is so obvious, it is easier to identify and buy into as the mission. However, this paradigm can be a trap that potentially may keep management focused on outdated products.

Charting a Strategic Course

Today, many products and services race through the business cycle and are obsolete or outmoded faster than products and services were in the past. For example, once there was only one long-distance telephone service. Now there are long distance "packages" for a range of customer types that, in turn, change their pricing, features, and names from month to month. By being very clear about what the organization stands for and why it exists, decision makers enhance their ability to think strategically about what the organization could do, as well as what it should not do.

Compare the stories of Zenith and Motorola. For many years, both companies were known for manufacturing televisions. While Zenith retained its focus on television manufacturing, Motorola changed from televisions to microprocessors—and then on to aggressively pursuing strategies to achieve its core purpose of providing integrated communication solutions and embedded electronic solutions. Motorola could give up what it made years ago when it did not fit the core purpose. Zenith could not.

Making Operational-Level Decisions

Mission statements, when they are written in terms of customer needs, also serve as a decision making and leadership tool for operational-level decisions. An example from the government sector illustrates this process. At first glance, a city fire department might define its mission based on what it does: put out fires. But a fire department's purpose goes beyond this definition. If a car is leaking gasoline, or if a parent calls to say his or her child stopped breathing, the fire department will respond and provide life-saving measures and emergency transportation to a hospital. Thus, a more realistic statement based on why the fire department exists would be to ensure the preparation of officers, men, women, and equipment "so that together we are prepared to provide cost-effective resolutions to emergencies that threaten or will threaten life and property in our community."

Given this new definition—or mission statement—of the city's fire department, suppose the department has limited funds and must choose between purchasing a ladder truck to increase the capabilities of the department and an equipment truck to carry new rescue tools. As part of the decision-making process, the team of firefighters reviews these two options against the statement.

First, the ladder truck: Does it improve the preparedness of the equipment? Yes.

Is it cost effective? Yes, as made evident by a review of the financial data.

Will it help to reduce the threat to lives and property? Yes. It will provide access to those who need rescue from upper floors.

The review continues. Then the equipment truck is compared in terms of its value in supporting the department's purpose. The advantage of this process is that the operational-level decision is based on clear facts and is linked to the organization's mission.

Similarly, at AT&T, the decision to add new products and services is based largely on the company's customer-oriented mission to bring people together and give them easy access to each other. How closely the proposed product or service achieves this mission determines whether it will be introduced or not.

Thus, in for-profit, nonprofit, and government organizations, a clearly defined purpose written from a customer-oriented perspective has two advantages. It provides a framework for charting an organization's strategic course, and it is a guide for operational-level decision making.

Philosophy and Values

The second key component of the mission statement defines the organization's philosophy—its basic beliefs, values, and priorities. These statements also provide guidelines for those within the company, particularly in terms of their behaviors, their conduct, how they intend to do business, and what kind of organization they want to build. An understanding of the organization's social responsibility is also spelled out.

A company whose values are legendary is Johnson & Johnson. This organization publishes a value statement—a *credo*—that expresses its belief that the company's first responsibility is to the doctors, nurses, and patients who use Johnson & Johnson products. Next come its employees, the communities in which the employees live and work, and finally the stockholders. The credo is displayed in every manager's office, and it guides making every important decision. To view a copy of the Johnson & Johnson credo, go to **http://www.jnj.com/home.htm**.

Exercise 1

How Well Do These Organizations Communicate Their Purpose?

INSTRUCTIONS

Review the mission statements of Harley-Davidson, Medtronic, Inc., and Continental Airlines in Table 1.2. Each provides a definition of the company's purpose. Circle the letter in questions 1–6 that most closely matches how you think the statements satisfy the criteria for defining the core purpose in terms of customer needs and how the statements express the organization's philosophy and values. Then, as a team, perform activities on Pages 16–17.

TABLE 1.2 SAMPLE MISSION STATEMENTS

Harley-Davidson	Continental Airlines
Mission	**Corporate Vision**
We fulfill dreams through the experience of motorcycling, by providing to motorcyclists and to the general public an expanding line of motorcycles and branded products and services in selected market segments.	To Be Recognized as the Best Airline in the Industry by Our Customers, Employees and Shareholders.

Medtronic, Inc.

Mission

- To contribute to human welfare by application of biomedical engineering in the research, design, manufacture, and sale of instruments or appliances that alleviate pain, restore health, and extend life.

- To direct our growth in the areas of biomedical engineering where we display maximum strength and ability; to gather people and facilities that tend to augment these areas; to continuously build on these areas through education and knowledge assimilation; to avoid participation in areas where we cannot make unique and worthy contributions.

- To strive without reserve for the greatest possible reliability and quality in our products; to be the unsurpassed standard of comparison and to be recognized as a company of dedication, honesty, integrity, and service.

- To make a fair profit on current operations to meet our obligations, sustain our growth, and reach our goals.

- To recognize the personal worth of employees by providing an employment framework that allows personal satisfaction in work accomplished, security, advancement opportunity, and means to share in the company's success.

- To maintain good citizenship as a company.

Harley-Davidson

1. How closely does the mission statement define Harley-Davidson's core purpose in terms of customer needs?

A	B	C
No core purpose discussed	Defines core purpose in terms of product/service provided	Defines core purpose very well in terms of customer needs

2. Are statements of the organization's philosophy and values included?

A	B	C
No statements of philosophy/values	Statements are vague	Clearly expresses corporate philosophy/values

Continental Airlines

3. How closely does the mission statement define Continental Airline's core purpose in terms of customer needs?

A	B	C
No core purpose discussed	Defines core purpose in terms of product/services provided	Defines core purpose very well in terms of customer needs

4. Are statements of the organization's philosophy and values included?

A	B	C
No statements of philosophy/values	Statements are vague	Clearly expresses corporate philosophy/ values

Medtronic, Inc.

5. How closely does the mission statement define Medtronic's core purpose in terms of customer needs?

A	B	C
No core purpose discussed	Defines core purpose in terms of product/service provided	Defines core purpose very well in terms of customer needs

6. Are statements of the organization's philosophy and values included?

A	B	C
No statements of philosophy/values	Statements are vague	Clearly expresses corporate philosophy/values

Team Activity
Mission Statement Revision

Names: _____

_____

1. Transfer each team member's ratings onto the charts below:

Team Member	Core Purpose			Philosophy and Values		
	Harley-Davidson	Continental Airlines	Medtronic, Inc.	Harley-Davidson	Continental Airlines	Medtronic, Inc.

2. Discuss the above individual ratings. Through consensus, develop a new team rating of an A, B, or C for each of the mission statements.

Core Purpose			Philosophy and Values		
Harley-Davidson	Continental Airlines	Medtronic, Inc.	Harley-Davidson	Continental Airlines	Medtronic, Inc.

3. Rewrite one of the company statements to incorporate an improved definition of the core purpose according to the customer needs criteria.

_____

_____

_____

4. Pick one of the company statements that could include more information regarding philosophy and values. Give examples of what might be included.

_____

_____

5. What other characteristics of the statements did your team notice/discuss?

_____

_____

_____

Exercise 2: Video
Create a Mission Statement for Caribou Coffee

INSTRUCTIONS

View the video titled "Caribou Coffee," which provides an overview of the Caribou Coffee Company. The company is headquartered in Minneapolis and has over 490 coffeehouses and 6,000 employees. The company is located in 16 states in the United States as well as in several countries. Create a mission statement for Caribou Coffee either in teams or on an individual basis.

1. With the look and feel of an Alaskan lodge, including knotty-pine cabinetry, a fire-place, and soft seating, Caribou Coffee continues to expand through company-owned stores and franchises. Write a definition of the core purpose of this company according to the customer needs criteria.

_____

_____

_____

_____

2. What philosophy and values should be included in the statement, based on the information in the video?

_____

_____

_____

_____

Exercise 3: Video

Create a Mission Statement for Fossil, Inc.

INSTRUCTIONS
View the video titled "Fossil," which provides an overview of the Fossil organization. Fossil started in 1984 as a watch company and has grown to a global business with a presence in over 70 countries. Create a mission statement for Fossil either in teams or on an individual basis.

1. The Fossil brand is well known throughout the world because of its distinctiveness. The company has added sunglasses, belts, handbags, and other small leather goods to its product line and continues to expand the business globally. Write a definition of the core purpose of this company according to the customer needs criteria.

_____

_____

_____

_____

_____

2. What key company values are discussed in the video to support the mission?

_____

_____

Strategy Session 4
The Board's Role in Corporate Governance

OBJECTIVE
This session develops an understanding of the key issues involved in the governance of a corporation. Typically, in the study of strategic management, the focus is on the role of the CEO. The board of directors has important roles to play as well, and an understanding of these roles provides a necessary element in understanding the corporation as a whole.

The focus in strategic management is always on the CEO. This individual is taken to represent the top management of the enterprise, charged with the formulation and implementation of strategy. However, the CEO is answerable to the owners of the enterprise, namely the shareholders. In a public limited company, the board of directors, which is elected to oversee the affairs of the corporation, represents the shareholders. Thus, an examination of the role of the board and the relationship of the CEO to the board are important for an understanding of the strategic management of the firm.

> The governing board of directors must be a board that represents no one except the basic long-term interests of the enterprise.
>
> —Peter F. Drucker

Board Roles

The board may be said to perform three roles in the governance of the firm:

1. **Control.** This role is internally focused and is derived from its position as representatives of the owners. Agency theory suggests that in a principal (shareholders)–agent (management) relationship, the agent's interests may diverge from that of the principal and need to be controlled. For example, management may pursue market share while the shareholders may want higher returns. Thus the board serves as a watchdog over management, a role that includes monitoring managerial competence and overseeing resource allocation.

2. **Service.** This role has an external focus and considers the board as a *boundary spanner*. That is, it serves to connect the organization to its environment by providing information to management on the one hand, and represent the firm to the community on the other. As suggested by stakeholder theory, the board enhances the firm's legitimacy in society.

3. **Strategy.** This role is more recent in origin. Institutional theory suggests that organizations develop an inner logic of their own and seek a position and purpose different from that of those who control them. For example, some influential groups of shareholders may be looking for short-term appreciation of share prices and not for long-term competitive advantage. Thus, this theory argues that the board needs to think in terms of the long-term strategy of an enterprise, even though it may not

always serve the purpose of the diverse group of owners, some of whom may seek short-term rewards.

In seeking to perform these three roles, different boards have taken different paths. Some boards are activists and others are more passive. During the late 1980s and early 1990s, several large corporations in the United States went through a difficult period of governance that led to disagreements between the board and the CEO. At various times, the CEOs of General Motors, IBM, Kmart, Goodyear Tire & Rubber Co., Abbott Laboratories, and Greyhound Lines, among others, have quit over differences with their boards on how to run their respective organizations. A study by consulting firm Booz Allen found that 31.6% of CEOs worldwide who stepped down from office did so due to conflicts with their board.

The 1990s also saw scandals in major U.S. corporations such as Enron, WorldCom, and Tyco, which were related to accounting irregularities or financial mismanagement. As a response, the U.S. Congress passed the Sarbanes-Oxley Act in July 2002 that established the Public Accounting Oversight Board. The Oversight Board requires public companies to create and document new internal financial control systems, add independent directors, strengthen the role of audit committees, and make executive officers personally certify the accuracy of financial documents. Stock exchanges around the world have also put down guidelines on corporate governance for their listed companies.

The focus of most regulatory efforts and guidelines on governance is on better control and the expectation that the board would play a supervisory role. This has led boards to require a better working relationship with their CEOs and the desire to be kept informed about major plans of the company and variations in performance. The old era of boards rubber-stamping management decisions seems to be changing.

Independent guidelines exist in the United States **(www.nacdonline.org)** and in Europe **(www.ecgi.org)** in order to encourage good governance practices. Many large companies have devised their own set of guidelines on governance. These go beyond accounting or financial matters and typically include advice on becoming active participants and decision makers in the boardroom and not merely passive advisers. The guidelines also stress director independence, limiting the number of board memberships, and requiring members to immerse themselves in the company's business and industry.

Exercise

Translating the Board's Role into Guidelines for Practice

INSTRUCTIONS
PART I: BOARD GUIDELINES
The following are a selection of the 38 items in the guidelines that were adopted by the Board of Directors of General Motors, a U.S.-based automotive company. These guidelines were first set in 1994 and most recently revised in May 2007. For each item, assign one or more of the three roles (Control, Service, and Strategy) that seem to most closely relate to the activity by checking the appropriate box(es).

GM Board Guidelines

The General Motors Board of Directors represents the owners' interest in perpetuating a successful business, including optimizing long-term financial returns. The Board is responsible for determining that the Corporation is managed in such a way to ensure this result.... The Board's responsibility is to regularly monitor the effectiveness of management policies and decisions including the execution of its strategies.... [T]he Board has a responsibility to GM's customers, employees, suppliers and to the communities where it operates—all of whom are essential to a successful business.

Selection and Composition of the Board

1. *Board Membership Criteria*
   The Directors and Corporate Governance Committee is responsible for reviewing with the Board, on an annual basis, the appropriate skills and characteristics required of Board members in the context of the current makeup of the Board. Board candidates are evaluated based upon various criteria, such as their broad-based business skills and experiences, ethical standards, special skills, concern for the stockholders and other stakeholders, and a global business and social perspective, personal integrity, and judgment. In addition, directors must have significant time available to devote to Board activities and to enhance their knowledge of GM and the global automotive industry.

Control	Service	Strategy

2. *Selection of New Directors and Orientation*
   The Board itself is responsible for selecting its own members. The Board delegates the screening process involved to the Directors and Corporate Governance Committee with input from the Chairman and the Chief Executive Officer. The Board and management conduct a comprehensive orientation process for new Directors to become familiar with the Corporation's vision, strategic direction, core values, financial matters, and corporate governance practices.

Control	Service	Strategy

Board Leadership

3. *Selection of Chairman and CEO*

   The Board should be free to make this choice any way that seems best for the corporation at a given point in time. Therefore, the Board does not have a policy, one way or the other, on whether or not the role of the Chairman and Chief Executive Officer should be separate or combined and, if it is to be separate, whether the Chairman should be selected from the non-employee Directors or be an employee.

Control	Service	Strategy

4. *Chair of the Directors and Corporate Governance Committee*

   The Chair of the Directors and Corporate Governance Committee is an independent Director and acts as the Presiding Director for the Executive sessions of the independent Directors and in communicating the Board's annual evaluation of the Chairman and Chief Executive Officer.

Control	Service	Strategy

Board Composition and Performance

5. *Mix of Management and Independent Directors*

   The Board believes that there should be a substantial majority of independent Directors on the GM Board. Senior executives other than the Chairman and Chief Executive Officer currently attend Board meetings on a regular basis even though they are not members of the Board.

Control	Service	Strategy

6. *Board Definition of What Constitutes Independence for Directors*

   The Board is made up of a substantial majority of Directors who qualify as independent. [This is one who does not have a material relationship with GM, neither he/she nor immediate family members has been employed by GM, its auditors, or significant supplier/customer in the past three years.]

Control	Service	Strategy

7. *Former Chairman and Chief Executive Officer Board Membership*

   The Board believes that it is preferable that the Chairman and Chief Executive Officer not continue to serve on the Board following retirement from GM.

Control	Service	Strategy

8. *Term Limits and Retirement Age*

   The Board does not believe it should establish term limits. As an alternative to term limits, the Directors and Corporate Governance Committee in conjunction with the Chairman and Chief Executive Officer will formally review each Director's continuation on the Board every five years. This also allows each Director the opportunity to conveniently confirm his/her desire to continue as a member of the Board.

Control	Service	Strategy

9. *Assessing the Board's Performance*

   The Board performs a self-evaluation on an annual basis. The Directors and Corporate Governance Committee is responsible to report annually to the Board an assessment of the Board's performance. The assessment includes a review of the Board's overall effectiveness and the areas in which the Board or management believes the Board can make an impact on the Corporation. The purpose of the evaluation is to increase the effectiveness of the Board, not to focus on the performance of individual Board members.

Control	Service	Strategy

Board Relationship to Senior Management

10. *Ethics and Conflicts of Interest*

    The Board expects all Directors, as well as officers and employees, to act ethically at all times and to adhere to GM's policies. The Board will not permit any waiver of any ethics policy for any Director or executive officer.

Control	Service	Strategy

11. *Board Access to Senior Management*

    Board members have complete access to GM's Management. It is assumed that Board members will use judgment to be sure that this contact is not distracting to the business operation of the Corporation and that such contact, if in writing, be copied to the Chairman and Chief Executive Officer.

Control	Service	Strategy

Meeting Procedures

12. *Selection of Agenda Items for Board Meetings*

    The Chairman and Chief Executive Officer establishes the agenda for each Board meeting. Each Board member may suggest the inclusion of item(s) on the agenda.

Control	Service	Strategy

Committee Matters

13. *Board Committees*

    Membership on the Audit, Directors and Corporate Governance, Executive Compensation, Investment Funds, and Public Policy Committees consists only of independent Directors. All Committee charters are available on the Corporation's Web site.

Control	Service	Strategy

Leadership Development

14. *Formal Evaluation of the Chairman and Chief Executive Officer*

    The independent directors annually conduct a formal evaluation of the Chairman and Chief Executive Officer which is communicated to [him/her] by the presiding director. The evaluation should be based on objective criteria including performance of the business, accomplishment of long-term strategic objectives, development of management, etc. The evaluation is used by the Executive Compensation Committee.

Control	Service	Strategy

Questions

1. Which role has the maximum and which has the minimum coverage in the guidelines? Why is this so?

_____

_____

_____

_____

2. Do any of the items infringe on what you would consider top management's prerogative in running the company?

_____

_____

_____

_____

3. Are there any areas of governance of a corporation not considered in these guidelines? Write a statement that can be added to the guidelines.

_____

_____

_____

_____

PART II: ENRON BOARD
Review Enron Corporation's board and evaluate its effectiveness from the perspective of corporate governance in general, and GM's guidelines in particular.

Enron Corporation, a Houston, Texas-based energy company, filed for protection and reorganization under Chapter 11 of the Bankruptcy Code on December 2, 2002 **(www.enron.com)** and is under liquidation. The crisis in Enron began in October 2001, when it announced a restatement of earnings of about $600 million dating back to 1997. Subsequent revelations and the report of the Board's own Special Investigation Committee brought to light the following:

- Many Special Purpose Entities (SPEs) were created to conduct off-balance sheet transactions. They allowed the company to conceal losses from the public. These SPEs were run by employees who personally benefited in violation of the company's code of ethics. The Board had specifically suspended the code, at the recommendation of the Finance Committee, in order to approve the transactions.

- The Board's efforts at control were not adequate and those controls that were set up were not adequately implemented.

- The Board assigned the Audit and Compliance Committee an expanded duty to review the transactions, but the Committee carried them out only in a cursory way.

- The Board was denied important information that might have led it to take action, but the Board also did not appreciate the significance of some of the specific information that came before it.

- The Audit Committee did not object to Enron's legal advisors, Vinson & Elkins, investigating the complaints of a whistleblower, although she cautioned in the same letter against using the legal advisors because they had endorsed some of the SPEs.

Table 4.1 lists the names of the directors as of February 1, 2002. The year in parentheses is when the director joined the board. Review the list and respond to the question that follows.

TABLE 4.1   BOARD MEMBERS OF ENRON CORPORATION

Name (year appointed)	Title and Committee Membership	Other Information
Kenneth L. Lay (1985)	Chairman & CEO Executive Committee	
Robert A. Belfer (1983)	Executive and Finance Committees	CEO of Belfer Management, a private investment firm. Founded Belco Oil & Gas Corp., which, in 1997, bought a stake in another energy company from JEDI (an Enron SPE). JEDI used part of the funds ($140 million) to start Chewco, another SPE.
Norman P. Blake (1993)	Finance and Compensation Committees	Chairman, president, and CEO of Comdisco, Inc., an IT services company.
Ronnie C. Chan (1996)	Audit and Finance Committees	Chairman of Hang Lung Group, a properties-holding company in Hong Kong. Missed more than 25% of board meetings in 1996, 1997, and 2000. Missed 75% of the meetings in 2001.
John H. Duncan (1985)	Executive Committee Chair, Compensation Committee	Former chairman of Executive Committee, Gulf+Western Industries, a conglomerate.
Wendy L. Gramm (1993)	Audit and Nominating Committees	Director of Regulatory Studies Program, Mercatus Center, George Mason University. Former chairperson of Commodities Futures Trading Commission (CFTC). Enron's trading in energy derivatives was made exempt from regulation by the CFTC. Shortly after this decision, Ms. Gramm quit CFTC and joined the Enron board. By a special resolution of the board, her compensation was delinked from Enron's stock. Enron gave Mercatus Center $50,000 since 1996.
Robert K. Jaedicke (1985)	Audit Committee Chair, Compensation Committee	Accounting professor (emeritus) and former dean of Stanford University, School of Business. Seconded the motion suspending Enron's Code of Ethics.
Charles A. Lemaistre (1985)	Compensation Committee Chair, Executive Committee	President (emeritus) of MD Andersen Cancer Center, University of Texas, Houston, Texas. Predecessor of John Mendelsohn (see below).
John Mendelsohn (1999)	Audit and Nominating Committees	President of MD Andersen Cancer Center, University of Texas, Houston, Texas. Enron and related entities have donated $1,564,928 to MD Andersen Center since 1985.

(CONT)

TABLE 4.1   BOARD MEMBERS OF ENRON CORPORATION (CONT.)

Name (year appointed)	Title and Committee Membership	Other Information
Paulo V. Ferraz Pereira (1999)	Audit and Finance Committees	CEO of Meridional Financial Group, a financial holding company, Brazil. Former President and CEO of State Bank of Rio de Janeiro.
William C. Powers (2001)	Head of the Special Investigating Committee of the Board in 2001	Dean of University of Texas Law School. Member of University of Texas Capital Campaign Committee. Enron gave $3 million to the University and $250,000 to the Law School since he had become dean. Enron's law firm, Vinson and Elkins, endowed a chair at the Law School. Enron's General Counsel, James Derrick, was a trustee of the Law School Foundation until 2001.
Frank Savage (1999)	Finance and Compensation Committees	Chairman of Alliance Capital Management, investment management firm.
Raymond Troubh (2001)		A former investment banker and financial consultant. A director of 11 public companies.
John Wakeham (1994)	Nominating Committee Chair, Audit Committee	Member of House of Lords, United Kingdom. Chairman, Press Complaints Commission. Former Minister for Energy, United Kingdom. In that capacity he helped privatize the electricity industry and gave consent for Enron to build the country's largest power plant at Teeside. Was paid $72,000 a year since fall 1996 for services as a consultant to Enron's European unit.
Herbert S. Winokur Jr. (1985)	Finance Committee Chair, Executive Committee	Chairman and CEO of Capricorn Holdings, a private investment company. Director, Natco Group, which was a supplier to Enron and its subsidiaries. Finance Committee recommended suspension of the code of ethics.

1. On a separate sheet, evaluate the quality of the board. Could any of GM's guidelines have improved the governance at Enron? Can you suggest any new guideline? With the available information, which role(s) is each director best equipped to perform?

Strategy Session 5

Viewing Strategy from the Stakeholder Perspective

OBJECTIVE

This session illustrates the influence and claims of various stakeholder groups. In the exercises that follow the introductory reading, identify the stakeholders—and demonstrate how stakeholder interests and power are part of the strategy process.

Stakeholders are the individuals and groups who have the potential to influence the performance of an organization and who are impacted by the firm's strategies. The traditional concept of business gives supreme importance to the role and interests of the investors or *stock*holders. However, the concept of *stake*holders provides a useful alternative formulation for understanding how numerous organizations, groups, and individuals affect and are affected by a company's strategies and its performance. Examples of stakeholders in a company include customers and, of course, stockholders. However, employees, creditors, suppliers, governments—and the local community—are stakeholders in the company as well. Starbucks, the coffee store chain based in Seattle, is a good example of a company that identifies stakeholders beyond the organization. Its "Starbucks Gives Back" policy states that people "... at all levels of the company support Starbucks' guiding principle to contribute positively to our communities and our environment."

> The stakeholder approach is about groups and individuals who can affect the organization, and is about managerial behavior taken in response to those groups and individuals.
>
> —*R. E. Freeman*

The relationship of an organization with its stakeholders can be viewed as one of mutual interdependence. Customers provide the organizations with revenue in exchange for products and services. Stockholders buy shares and thus provide capital in exchange for a return on their investment. Employees provide the skills and labor and get income, good working conditions, and job satisfaction. Creditors provide loans and in exchange receive interest payments. Suppliers provide the inputs and receive payment for the inputs. Governments set rules and regulations that maintain fair competition and in exchange expect companies to adhere to the rules. The local community provides an infrastructure and expects the organization to be a socially responsible citizen.

Although managers must view the impact of these relationships when developing strategy, an organization cannot always satisfy the claims of all of its stakeholders. This is particularly the case when the goals of different groups conflict. For example, the local community may ask for a percentage of profits to be donated to local causes. However, stockholders might expect dividends to be paid from extra profits. Alternatively, employees may demand higher wages, while customers look for lower prices.

Because of these potential conflicts, managers are compelled to identify and prioritize stakeholders. The ultimate goal is to develop strategies that assure the achievement of organizational goals while maintaining positive stakeholder relations.

Exercise 1

Wal-Mart and Banking

INSTRUCTIONS
Read this summary about the Wal-Mart strategy to move into the banking industry. Then complete the following form to identify stakeholders and their influence in the formulation of this strategy.

The Wal-Mart Banking Strategy

Since the early 2000s, Wal-Mart has been on the move to provide financial products to a segment of the population defined as "underbanked." These are customers who have little to no access to banking services through traditional banks. Wal-Mart provides this segment with bargain-priced money orders and wire transfers. Through a partnership with Money-Gram International, immigrants can send money to their home countries from a Wal-Mart store. Because customer deposits are not accepted, Wal-Mart can provide these financial services without a bank charter or federal deposit insurance.

In fact, since the 1950s, the U.S. Congress enacted several laws that maintain the separation of commerce and banking and gave the Federal Reserve Board the power to limit the scope of activities undertaken by commercial firms that offer financial services. One reason for maintaining the separation is to avoid situations where retail firms may be tempted to draw on the financial subsidiary if the retail division has financial problems. Examples such as Enron illustrate the difficulty faced by federal regulators and market professionals to identify and evaluate transactions that may be disguised by complex financial structures. Another reason is that widespread ownership of banks by commercial firms would likely increase the necessity of federal regulators to provide financial support to a commercial firm if the financial entity is threatened with failure. A recent example is the Federal Reserve Board's rescue of Bear Stearns. Evidence from other countries also illustrates the issues that arise when linkages between banks and commercial firms exist. During the 1990s the major financial crises that occurred in Japan, South Korea, and Mexico were due in part to the conflicts of interest, preferential lending, and distorted economic incentives that resulted from ownership and control connections that existed between the banks and commercial firms.

However, despite the regulations that keep commerce and banking separate, there is a loophole that allows for the acquisition of an Industrial Loan Company (ILC). ILCs are state-chartered quasi-banks that were originally designed a century ago to help low-income workers get inexpensive loans. ILCs chartered under Utah law may use the title "bank" in their name and may offer most of the services of a state-chartered commercial bank. Currently, there are 15 ILCs owned by commercial firms.

When Wal-Mart applied in July 2005 for permission to establish Wal-Mart Bank as an ILC from Utah, a highly publicized battle began about whether Congress should stop acquisitions of ILCs. Wal-Mart's application was opposed by groups that included the Federal Reserve Board, members of Congress, community bankers, labor unions, and community activists. The Federal Reserve Board and Congress were concerned about risks to the U.S. financial system and the broader economy and about the lack of adequate supervisory powers to monitor and control ILCs. Concerns were voiced by community bankers and the Independent Community Bankers of America, an industry advocacy group. In their viewpoint Wal-Mart was using the ILC charter approach as a back door to get into the retail-banking industry. Some banks argued that they were not able to get into real-estate brokerage because of the separation between commerce and banking, so the commercial firms should not be granted ILC charters. Labor unions voiced concerns about Wal-Mart's reputation as being strongly anti-union and about its policies, such as cutthroat employment practices. Wal-Mart Watch, a labor-backed activist group that seeks to change Wal-Mart's business practices, argued for states to bar the opening of branches inside the affiliate's stores. The result would be less revenue from financial services.

When Home Depot, the second-largest U.S. retailer, requested permission in May 2006 to acquire EnerBank, an existing Utah-chartered ILC, all applications were put on hold until January 31, 2008, so that Congress could review the risks to the U.S. financial system and could examine regulation of ILCs. No further action was taken through 2008, since the attention of Congress has been diverted by the subprime lending crisis; and both Wal-Mart and Home Depot have withdrawn their applications for ILCs.

Wal-Mart has plans for new financial services in lieu of the ILC charter. According to statements by company officials, revenues from its financial services operations are increasing 30% annually; and the company has plans to carve out store space for its existing services among other opportunities. One former employee noted that while Wal-Mart has been held off in its attempts to get into the banking industry, the company will eventually succeed … and bankers may not be ready for what will hit them.

Wal-Mart's Banking Strategy

1. After reading the information about Wal-Mart's bid to enter the banking industry, what is your opinion of this strategic move?

_____

_____

2. Identify the stakeholders of Wal-Mart. List them according to the level of influence they exert over the company, showing the stakeholder with the highest level first, then the stakeholder with the next highest level of influence, and so on. The last stakeholder on the list should be the one with the lowest level of influence. Next to each, briefly discuss the reasons behind your ranking.

Stakeholder Listing	Brief Discussion of Stakeholder Influence/Power

Exercise 2

Role Playing Global Chemical Stakeholders' Interests and Power

Global Chemical Company

Several years ago, a citizen environmental group from Kentucky began complaining about the health hazards they claimed were being carried downstream from the processing facility of Global Chemical across the state border in Ashton, West Virginia. Several small towns along the river in Kentucky had been affected by the pollution. They brought in health specialists to support their claims that pollutants from the river were causing serious health problems in these towns.

An independent study conducted by the state of West Virginia concluded that while the residents of these towns did experience higher-than-normal levels of a number of types of cancer, "there is no proven link between these diseases and the chemicals from Global."

Now, despite this lack of proof, it appears that Global Chemical's board of directors will consider the charges against the facility at its next meeting.

As part of the materials to be sent to board members, the CEO would like to include recommendations about what action to take on this problem. The filtering system is too old to be upgraded, and to put in a new system would cost millions and would close the plant for months. Some board members think it would make more sense to build a new plant somewhere else (maybe overseas, where environmental laws are not as strict) rather than put an entirely new filtering system in such an old facility.

Further complicating the situation is the fact that almost half of the workers in this community work at Global. Closing the plant for even a few months not only would cause extreme financial hardship but also would threaten the existence of many local businesses. Understandably, the unions at the company are totally opposed to any actions that might hurt their members, especially since none of the pollution charges have been proven.

The citizens' environmental group from Kentucky is threatening to cooperate with a *60Minutes*-type program that is going to develop an exposé of the situation on national television. If it gets to that point, it might not matter that there is no proof that the chemicals from Global cause the diseases found in the Kentucky towns.

Global Chemical Case: Preassessment

1. After reading the Global Chemical case, what strategy should Global Chemical pursue at this time and why?

_____

_____

_____

2. Identify the stakeholders of Global Chemical. List them according to the level of influence they exert over the company, showing the stakeholder with the highest level first, then the stakeholder with the next highest level of influence, and so on. The last stakeholder on the list should be the one with the lowest level of influence. Next to each, briefly discuss the reasons behind your ranking.

Stakeholder Listing	Brief Discussion of Stakeholder Influence/Power

Team Activity
Stakeholder Group

Names: _____

_____

You will be assigned to a stakeholder group. Each group develops a specific position on what Global Chemical's strategy should be while management formulates its strategic plan.

1. Each stakeholder group should select one person to act as spokesperson while the management team should divide responsibilities among its various members (30 to 40 minutes for steps 1 and 2).

2. The entire class reconvenes with each stakeholder group staying intact. The Global Chemical management team presents its plan and answers any questions of clarification. Then the stakeholder groups huddle individually for 5 minutes to review their positions in light of the Global Chemical presentation. A spokesperson from each group gives a brief response to the strategic plan. The management in turn is allowed to respond in a very brief manner. The board of directors should have the final say in its role as the group to which management is primarily accountable. Once all of the stakeholder groups have presented, a question and answer period directed to the management team is in order (40 to 45 minutes).

3. A second brief round of meetings takes place. Global Chemical's management team should reassess its strategic plan in light of the critiques by various groups. Each stakeholder group should discuss its position in relationship to the corporation as well as other stakeholder groups (10 minutes).

4. The entire class reconvenes. Global Chemical management presents any changes in its strategic plan. Each stakeholder is given an opportunity to make a brief statement. The board of directors should have the final say (10 to 15 minutes).

Strategy Session 6

Forces Affecting Competitive Strategy   37

Exercise: Intensity of Competition in the Casino Gambling Industry   39

Strategy Session 7

Generating a Plan of Action: SWOT (TOWS) Analysis   47

Exercise 1: An Action Plan for Robin Hood   49

Exercise 2: Video—Kropf Fruit Company—Future Strategy   53

Strategy Session 8

Developing Generic Strategy   55

Exercise 1: Choosing How to Compete in the Lodging Industry   57

Exercise 2: Video—The Generic Strategy of Fossil, Inc.   60

Strategy Session 9

Build Your Competitive Advantage   61

Exercise: Build Your Intended Strategy   63

Strategy Session 10

Viewing Corporate Strategy from the Core Competencies Perspective   65

Exercise: Corporate Strategy at Honda   67

Strategy Session 11

Global Strategic Alliances   71

Exercise: Renewing the General Motors–Toyota Alliance   73

Strategy Session 12

Identifying Transnational Strategies   79

Exercise: Global Operations of Bata Shoe and Nike   81

Strategy Session 13

Understanding Turnaround Management   87

Exercise: The Decline–Turnaround Sequence   89

Strategy Session 14

Scenario Planning: Innovative Approaches for the Future   93

Exercise: Develop Some Scenarios   95

PART II

Designing Strategy

Strategy Session 6
Forces Affecting Competitive Strategy

OBJECTIVE

This session will help identify the forces of competition and determine what effects these forces have on a competitor's ability to earn high profits. The exercise features a profile of the casino gambling industry that lets you assess these forces.

An *industry* is defined as the group of competitors that produce similar products or services that satisfy the same basic consumer need. For example, the lodging industry consists of hotels and motels that compete with one another to provide accommodation for travelers away from home. The automobile industry consists of competitors that manufacture and market cars, trucks, and other kinds of vehicles to transport people, property, and services.

> Most of us never recognize opportunity until it goes to work in our competitor's business.
>
> —*P. L. Andarr*

Managers must understand the nature of competition within their industry so that they can identify opportunities and threats facing the company. From this analysis, they judge the potential in the industry for above-normal profitability and ultimately determine the best strategy for the firm to pursue to either offset or influence competitive forces. The model for analyzing an industry consists of five forces of competition developed by Michael Porter:

1. **Industry Competition—Rivalry Among Existing Firms.** When companies in the same industry compete, they often use tactics such as price competition, new product introduction, and advertising slogans and campaigns. The intensity of the competition depends on factors such as the number of competitors, rate of industry growth, amount of fixed costs, product or service characteristics, exit barriers, capacity levels, and the diversity of rivals.

2. **Threat of New Entrants.** New entrants or companies that are not currently part of the competitive group may be looking for an opportunity to enter the industry. How much of a threat they pose depends on the barriers to entry present and the reaction from existing competitors. Barriers to entry include economies of scale, product differentiation, capital requirements, cost disadvantages independent of size, access to distribution channels, and government policy.

3. **Bargaining Power of Suppliers.** Suppliers to an industry are those who supply materials and services required by firms in the industry. Suppliers can affect the profitability of an industry if they are able to raise prices or reduce the quality of purchased goods or services. Forces affecting supplier bargaining power include the number of available suppliers, the uniqueness of a supplier's product or service, whether the industry competitor has the potential of integrating backward to produce the supplier's product, the cost to change suppliers, and whether the industry is an important customer of the supplier.

4. **Bargaining Power of Buyers.** Buyers are usually consumers of the product or service, but they can also include wholesalers and retailers who bring the product to the consumer. Buyers affect an industry by being able to force down prices, bargain for more services, or play competitors against each other. Typically, industrial or commercial buyers have bargaining power when they purchase in large volume or when the costs of switching from one industry player to another are low. Consumer buyers tend to be more price-sensitive when they purchase undifferentiated products or when the products are expensive relative to their income.

5. **Threat of Substitute Products and Services.** Substitute products are those provided by competitors in a different industry but come close to satisfying the same consumer need. For example, renting videos or DVDs is a substitute for going to the movies, wine is a substitute for beer, and so on. The threat of substitutes exists because their existence places a ceiling on prices the industry can charge. When prices get too high, consumers will switch to the substitute, unless the industry upgrades or differentiates its product, thus making the substitute less appealing.

Other scholars have suggested the following two additional forces for inclusion in an industry analysis.

1. **Relative Power of Other Stakeholders.** Other stakeholders, such as local communities, creditors, trade associations, governments, special-interest groups, and stockholders can exert powerful influence on the industry and affect the nature of competition.

2. **Power of Complementors.** A *complementor* is defined as an industry whose product works with the product of the industry being analyzed and without which the industry's product would lose much of its value. An example can be found in the microprocessor industry, in which companies in the software industry are seen as complementors.

In scanning the industry, management assesses each force as high, medium, or low in terms of its strength and judges the potential for above normal profitability in the industry. While a high force is a threat because it is likely to reduce profits, a low force is an opportunity because it may allow the company to raise prices and earn higher profits. Thus, studying each force points management to actions that it can take to influence the effect of the industry's forces on the company.

Exercise

Intensity of Competition in the Casino Gambling Industry

INSTRUCTIONS

Read the description of the casino gambling industry below. Respond to the questions that follow in order to evaluate the intensity of the forces and their impact on the profitability that can be attained in the industry.

The Casino Gambling Industry in the United States: Expansion and Competition

Compared to industries such as the traditional hotel business, the gambling industry is not mature. Up until 1988, legal casinos operated in only New Jersey (Atlantic City) and Nevada. During the 1990s, gambling revenues increased largely as a result of geographical expansion into the Midwest and the South and to new investment in Las Vegas. Today more than 20 states allow gambling. In fact, much of the industry's expansion is due to casinos being allowed on Native American land in various states.

The casino gambling industry includes more than 450 legal casinos in the United States that offer customers the opportunity to play coin-fed machines and table games. This industry group does not include facilities that focus on bingo, or other facilities such as racetracks in Delaware and Iowa, where casino activity is limited to coin-fed machines. Revenues, which are the amount of money wagered less the winnings paid to players, totaled approximately $58.7 billion in 2007.

Table 6.1 shows a breakdown of facilities and revenues by location.

TABLE 6.1 CASINO GAMBLING FACILITIES AND REVENUES BY STATE, 2007

Location	Number of Facilities	Revenues
Nevada (statewide)	274 casinos in addition to smaller facilities, such as taverns and retail stores, with video poker machines.	$12.8 billion
Atlantic City, NJ	11 high-volume casinos	$4.9 billion
Mississippi, Indiana, Illinois, Louisiana, Missouri, and Iowa waterways	83 water casino projects (some consisting of more than one casino boat)	$11.8 billion
Detroit, MI New Orleans, LA Colorado; Deadwood, SD	3 casinos 1 land-based casino 50 limited stakes casinos	$2.7 billion

Note: The remainder of industry revenues is from casinos on Native American land.

Although more than 20 states allow gambling, the industry is highly regulated, and the introduction of casino activity requires licenses or agreements with state authorities. A significant form of regulation is taxation. In some markets, the state or local tax on casino winnings may be less than 10%, while in other markets it exceeds 20%.

The casino industry faced its steepest slump in 2008 due to the recessionary economy and the tough financing environment. The housing market decline and concerns about unemployment affected consumer discretionary income. A reliance on revenue from conferences and conventions also increased the industry's sensitivity to the economy.

Native American Casinos

The Native American Gaming Regulatory Act of 1988 gave Native American tribes the right to negotiate for the development of a gaming facility. Based on data from the federal regulatory agency known as the National Indian Gaming Commission, more than 200 of approximately 550 Native American tribes in the United States own and/or operate casinos in the nation. The highest volume projects are on Mohegan and Mashantucket Pequot land in Connecticut.

The growth of Native American-owned gaming creates opportunities for other casino companies to provide management services. Although outsiders cannot own Native American gambling facilities, they are allowed to manage properties under contract.

Variation in Casinos

In the United States, individual states have the power to grant new casino gambling licenses and to regulate the industry. Because of the diverse state regulations, there is considerable variation in the appearance, scope, and location of new casinos. In some states, projects have developed in stages. A boat with gambling can be opened quickly. As of year-end 2007, about 81 water-based casino projects were open in Iowa, Illinois, Mississippi, Louisiana, Missouri, and Indiana. After Hurricane Katrina, legislation was passed in Mississippi allowing casinos to be placed up to 800 feet inland from a high-point tide.

If the riverboat operation is favorable and if financing is available, a company can enlarge its gambling space and add related facilities, such as hotel rooms. Finding ways to differentiate casinos is an important competitive advantage, particularly since casino floors with slot machines and table games look alike. The Las Vegas Strip uses special themes and attractions to create different settings, such as ancient Egypt, a pirate ship, and a castle. Companies such as Harrah's Entertainment are developing strong brand recognition among customers. Proximity to interstate highways and major population centers is an advantage for new gaming facilities. Also, some companies target specific groups of customers. Boyd Gaming targets residents of Hawaii and operates six weekly charter flights from Honolulu to Las Vegas.

Abandoned Projects

Up until February 2008, low interest rates, high real estate values, and solid cash flow attracted many private equity deals in the gambling industry. However, the credit crunch resulted in Harrah's cancellation of a $2.1 billion resort in the Bahamas. In Las Vegas, foreclosure proceedings began on the Cosmopolitan. This project had estimated construction costs of $2 billion, and ended up with costs of $3.9 billion. Developments that need additional funding, such as the Las Vegas Sands project in Singapore, may also be put on hold.

Internet Gambling

The Unlawful Internet Gambling Enforcement Act of 2006 (UIGEA) was meant to force banks to block payments to gambling Web sites, and it required that the Federal Reserve and the Treasury Department issue regulations on identifying and blocking Internet gambling transactions. As of April 2008, the director of the Division of Reserve Bank Operations and Payment Systems noted that in recent years, card issuers and money transmitting businesses initiated steps that make funding for gambling on the Internet more difficult. However, some banks have concerns about their role in determining which transactions should be blocked under the law. The American Banking Association has complained that the law pushes banks to the position of policing illegal activities.

The European Union is launching an investigation of whether the law violates international trade rules. The EU trade commissioner suggested that the U.S. could be selectively enforcing the law against EU companies. Although Financial Services

Chairman Barney Frank proposed Internet Gambling HR 576, which would delay the implementation of the law until a definition of unlawful internet gambling was developed, the House Financial Services Committee rejected the bill on June 25, 2008. Thus, despite the issues associated with implementing UIGEA, the law will not be overturned.

Industry Structure

The U.S. casino gambling industry has become more consolidated over time due to acquisitions and internal growth. The largest company, ranked by casino winnings, is Harrah's Entertainment, Inc. This company was taken private in 2007.

China, however, is changing the structure of the industry. One of the world's hottest gambling markets is Macau, the only part of China where gambling is legal. The Macau casinos generated $3.71 billion in gambling revenue during the first three months of 2008, which is more than their counterparts in Las Vegas and Atlantic City combined. As a result, international properties, such as those in Macau, are changing the structure of the U.S. industry. This is similar to the situation that occurred with the automobile industry.

Gambling promoters for Galaxy Entertainment Group, one of six licensed casino companies in Macau, have become very aggressive in increasing the supply of VIP customers from mainland China. These mega-junkets are causing concern for casino operators such as Wynn Resorts, MGM Mirage, and Las Vegas Sands whose stock prices have declined in part because of increasing challenges they face doing business in Macau.

Suppliers

International Game Technology (IGT) designs, manufactures, and markets computerized gaming equipment, systems, and services. The company is the largest supplier of slot machines and is headquartered in Reno, Nevada; and the slot machine industry is highly concentrated. IGT business expansion has occurred through acquisitions and the development of strategic alliances. For example, in 2005 IGT acquired a Canadian distributor, a provider of Internet gaming technology, content, and services, and a provider of consulting services and technology in the gaming and hospitality market. In 2007, strategic agreements were established in the China lottery market.

Although casino revenues are expected to decline, gaming machine sales will increase due to a shift to server-based slot machines. This will result in demand for replacement equipment at casinos.

Transportation

For many of the larger gambling properties, customers arrive by airline, especially business and vacation travelers. Although fares for air travel rose substantially in 2007, airlines have offered fare sales. Automobiles are the primary means by which customers travel to casinos. The smaller, regional, and Native American gambling markets are negatively affected by the gasoline prices.

Activists

Although many residents of communities where commercial casinos are located support casino gambling, many other groups do not. Various churches, ad hoc citizens' groups, and national organizations such as the National Coalition Against Legalized Gambling protest legalized gambling because it comes with a high social cost in the form of addiction. They argue that youth are drawn into compulsive gambling habits at double the rate of adults, and that gambling has hidden negative economic impacts, such as diverting revenue that would be spent at local businesses. This, in turn, results in increased costs to the state from bankruptcies, addiction treatment centers, and the penal system. These organizations also point to the fact that when state governments depend on casinos for tax revenue, it puts the government in a compromised position. Government now has a vested interest in encouraging its citizens to lose money.

Casinos have attempted to address these concerns much like the alcohol companies that encourage responsible drinking. Most casinos post phone numbers for Gamblers Anonymous at their cashier windows and provide literature with information on problem gambling. Underage gambling is not allowed, and many casinos will not even permit minors in the gambling areas.

Complete the information below and identify the intensity of each of the forces of competition:

1. Rivalry Among Existing Firms   **High   Medium   Low**

   a) Define the casino gambling industry.

_____

_____

_____

   b) What is its level of concentration?

_____

_____

_____

2. Threat of New Entrants   **High   Medium   Low**

What are the barriers to entry into this industry?

_____

_____

_____

3. Bargaining Power of Suppliers   **High   Medium   Low**

   a) Who are the suppliers?

_____

_____

b) Discuss supplier bargaining power.

_____

_____

_____

4. Bargaining Power of Buyers   **High   Medium   Low**

a) Who are the buyers?

_____

_____

_____

b) Discuss whether the buyers have bargaining power.

_____

_____

_____

5. Threat of Substitutes   **High   Medium   Low**

What other substitutes limit the sales and profits for firms in this industry?

_____

_____

_____

6. Relative Power of Other Stakeholders   **High   Medium   Low**

Who are other major stakeholders?

_____

_____

_____

7. Relative Power of Complementors   **High   Medium   Low**

Who are the complementors?

_____

_____

_____

8. Now that you have analyzed each of the forces of competition, discuss the implications of the above levels of intensity.

   a) Which forces of competition are most threatening now? Which do you expect will change over the next, say, five years?

   _____

   _____

   _____

   b) What are the implications in terms of profit margins in this industry today? Over the next five years?

   _____

   _____

   _____

c)   As the CEO of a firm in this industry, what actions does this analysis suggest you implement in order to strengthen your competitive strategy?

_____

_____

_____

d)   As an advisor to a potential entrant, would you recommend entry? What steps would you advise them to take?

_____

_____

_____

Strategy Session 7

Generating a Plan of Action: SWOT (TOWS) Analysis

OBJECTIVE
The SWOT model provides a comprehensive view of the firm in relation to its environment. Taking this further, you will learn to build a plan of action using the TOWS matrix.

The term SWOT is widely used and well known in the field of strategic management. It is an acronym for **S**trengths, **W**eaknesses, **O**pportunities, and **T**hreats, and represents a helpful tool for generating a summary of a strategic situation. Strengths and weaknesses capture the internal environment of the firm and may include skills, expertise, organizational resources, competitive capabilities, positional advantages or disadvantages, weak finances, market share, brand recognition, or distribution capabilities, to name a few. Opportunities and threats stem from a company's external competitive environment. It represents trends in the environment that may be favorable or unfavorable to the firm. A merger of two rivals may, for example, be a threat. Or, increasing concern in society about convenience may be a favorable trend for a company whose products and services are designed for busy consumers. New regulations or the emergence of lower-cost technologies, on the other hand, may pose threats. The purpose of this classification was to ensure a good fit between the firm's material, technical, financial, and managerial resources to ensure full exploitation of opportunities while minimizing risks facing the firm.

> The strategic alternative, which results from matching opportunity and corporate capability at an acceptable level of risk, is what we may call an economic strategy.
>
> —*Kenneth R. Andrews, The Concept of Corporate Strategy*

By putting the four categories in a matrix format, Prof. H. Weihrich provided a useful tool to generate alternatives in a systematic manner. In this format, the analysis is referred to as the *TOWS matrix* (Figure 7.1 , shown in the following exercise). This enables one to match the elements of strengths and weaknesses with the opportunities and threats to generate action steps. When S and O are matched in the SO box, they represent possible ways in which the organization can use its strengths to take advantage of opportunities and favorable trends in the environment. Similarly, the ST box represents ways in which strengths could be used to protect the organization from threats. The WO suggests areas internally that need to be tackled to take advantage of the opportunities, and WT shows how the weaknesses make the organization most vulnerable against threats and thereby point to defensive tactics.

Take care in entering items in the S, W, O, and T boxes, for they determine the quality of action steps you will generate. Try to be as specific as you can. For instance, rather than saying "Good marketing skills," it is better to specify what aspect of marketing a company can do well. Or, instead of listing "International expansion" as an opportunity, try to spell out what market characteristic, internationally, represents the opportunity. When you match the items to generate action steps, state it as actions the organization can undertake, rather than as an analysis of the situation. Matching the strengths and opportunities directs the growth and expansion of firms. However, equally important is the intersection of weaknesses and threats. They represent areas where the organization is particularly vulnerable, especially in a very competitive environment. Steps the organization could take to mitigate potential threats and strengthen its position are important components of an action plan.

Complementary action steps, from the various boxes, can be combined to form a cohesive "alternative." When at least two such alternative groups of action steps are formed, they present alternative plans of action for the future. Then, depending on goals, resource availability, short vs. long-term time frame, etc., the organization can make a choice.

Exercise 1
An Action Plan for Robin Hood

INSTRUCTIONS

Read the "Robin Hood" case below. Look at Robin Hood and his band of Merry Men as an organization. Think of their activities and the issues that they face using management and business terms such as leadership, recruitment, revenue generation, expansion, diversification, competition, and the like.

1. Identify elements of their organizational strengths and weaknesses. Examine the external environment and identify trends that represent opportunities and threats. Enter the items identified in the appropriate places in the TOWS matrix in Figure 7.1 that follows the case.

2. Then match, one by one, the elements from the "Internal" axis (S or W) with ones from the "External" axis (O or T) and write them as action step (that is, actions the organization can undertake) at the intersections in the boxes labeled SO, WO, ST, and WT. Track the source of the ideas for the match within parenthesis. A brief example is given in the chart in Figure 7.1. Then answer questions 1 and 2 that follow.

Robin Hood

It was in the spring of the second year of his insurrection against the High Sheriff of Nottingham that Robin Hood took a walk in Sherwood Forest. As he walked, he pondered the progress of the campaign, the disposition of his forces, the Sheriff's recent moves, and the options that confronted him.

The revolt against the Sheriff had begun as a personal crusade. It erupted out of Robin's conflict with the Sheriff and his administration. However, alone Robin Hood could do little. He therefore sought allies, men with grievances and a deep sense of justice. Later he welcomed all who came, asking few questions and demanding only a willingness to serve. Strength, he believed, lay in numbers.

He spent the first year forging the group into a disciplined band, united in enmity against the Sheriff and willing to live outside the law. The band's organization was simple. Robin ruled supreme, making all important decisions. He delegated specific tasks to his lieutenants. Will Scarlett was in charge of intelligence and scouting. His main job was to shadow the Sheriff and his men, always alert to their next move. He also collected information on the travel plans of rich merchants and tax collectors. Little John kept discipline among the men, and saw to it that their archery was at the high peak that their profession demanded. Scarlock took care of the finances, converting loot to cash, paying shares of the take, and finding suitable hiding places for the surplus. Finally, Much, the Miller's son, had the difficult task of provisioning the ever increasing band of Merry Men.

The increasing size of the band was a source of satisfaction for Robin, but also a source of concern. The fame of his Merry Men was spreading, and new recruits poured in from every corner of England. As the band grew larger, their small bivouac became a major encampment. Between raids the men milled about, talking and playing games. Vigilance declined, and discipline was becoming harder to enforce. "Why," Robin reflected, "I don't know half the men I run into these days."

The growing band was also beginning to exceed the food capacity of the forest. Game was becoming scarce, and supplies had to be obtained from outlying villages. The cost of buying food was beginning to drain the band's financial reserves at the very moment when revenues were in decline. Travelers, especially those with the most to lose, were now giving the forest a wide berth. This was costly and inconvenient to them, but it was preferable to having all their goods confiscated.

Robin believed that the time had come for the Merry Men to change their policy of outright confiscation of goods to one of a fixed transit tax. His lieutenants strongly resisted this idea. They were proud of the Merry Men's famous motto "Rob from the rich and give to the poor." "The farmers and the townspeople," they argued, "are our most important allies. How can we tax them, and still hope for their help in our fight against the Sheriff?"

Robin wondered how long the Merry Men could keep to the ways and methods of their early days. The Sheriff was growing stronger and becoming better organized. He now had the money and the men and was beginning to harass the band, probing for its weaknesses. The tide of events was beginning to turn against the Merry Men. Robin felt that the campaign must be decisively concluded before the Sheriff had a chance to deliver a mortal blow. "But how," he wondered, "could this be done?"

Robin had often entertained the possibility of killing the Sheriff, but the chances for this seemed increasingly remote. Besides, killing the Sheriff might satisfy his personal thirst for revenge, but it would not improve the situation. Robin had hoped that the perpetual state of unrest, and the Sheriff's failure to collect taxes, would lead to his removal from office. Instead, the Sheriff used his political connections to obtain reinforcement. He had powerful friends at court and was well regarded by the regent, Prince John.

Prince John was vicious and volatile. He was consumed by his unpopularity among the people, who wanted the imprisoned King Richard back. He also lived in constant fear of the barons, who had first given him the regency, but were now beginning to dispute his claim to the throne. Several of these barons had set out to collect the ransom that would release King Richard the Lionheart from his jail in Austria. Robin was invited to join the conspiracy in return for future amnesty. It was a dangerous proposition. Provincial banditry was one thing, court intrigue another. Prince John had spies everywhere, and he was known for his vindictiveness. If the conspirators' plan failed, the pursuit would be relentless, and retributions swift.

The sound of the supper horn startled Robin from his thoughts. There was the smell of roasting venison in the air. Nothing was resolved or settled. Robin headed for camp promising himself that he would give these problems his utmost attention after tomorrow's raid.

FIGURE 7.1 TOWS MATRIX FOR "ROBIN HOOD"

INTERNAL

	Strengths (S) Size: more fighting men	**Weaknesses (W)**
Opportunities (O) *Favorable Trends* 1. Other forests available	**SO** 1. Expand operations to other forests (S1,O1)	**WO**
Threats (T) *Unfavorable Trends* 1. Game (food) becoming scarce	**ST** 1. Create separate group with a different mission—to hunt for food and not involved in robbing. (S1,T1)	**WT**

EXTERNAL

1. The boxes SO, WO, ST, and WT contain individual action steps. Combine them into at least two categories that represent alternative courses of action. List the two alternatives and their constituent action steps below.

_____

_____

_____

_____

_____

_____

_____

2. What criteria will you use to choose between the alternatives listed above?

_____

_____

_____

_____

_____

_____

_____

Exercise 2: Video

Kropf Fruit Company——Future Strategy

INSTRUCTIONS

View the video titled "Kropf Fruit Company" which provides a description of the challenges facing a small/medium-sized grower.

1. Note the organization's strengths and weaknesses, opportunities, and threats as presented. Do you agree? Enter the items identified in the appropriate places in Figure 7.2, the blank TOWS matrix on the next page.

2. Next, one by one, match the elements from the "Internal" axis (S or W) with ones from the "External" axis (O or T) and write them as action steps (that is, actions the organization can undertake) in the inside boxes labeled SO, WO, ST, and WT. Then answer questions provided by your instructor.

FIGURE 7.2   TOWS MATRIX FOR "KROPF FRUIT COMPANY"

INTERNAL

	Strengths (S)	**Weaknesses (W)**
Opportunities (O) *Favorable Trends*	SO	WO
Threats (T) *Unfavorable Trends*	ST	WT

EXTERNAL

Strategy Session 8
Developing Generic Strategy

OBJECTIVE
In this session, consider the advantages of generic strategy and then compare organizations in the exercise—ones that pursue each of the four kinds of generic strategies—and a firm that is stuck in the middle.

Organizations develop a business-level strategy by using company resources and distinctive competencies to gain a competitive advantage over rivals in an industry. Michael Porter, who developed the framework for business-level strategy, labeled it *generic strategy* because in principle the choices of strategy can be applied to any business and any industry.

Generic strategy choices involve two dimensions: competitive advantage and competitive scope. In seeking competitive advantage, a company might choose a low-cost strategy when trying to outperform other firms in a particular industry. This strategy is the ability of a company to design, produce, and market a product more efficiently and at a lower cost than its competitors. Alternatively, a company might choose a differentiation strategy as a means of gaining competitive advantage. Differentiation is the ability to provide products or services that are perceived to be unique by customers and for which they are willing to pay more. For example, Maytag produces washers and other household appliances that consumers pay more for because they are perceived to be of better quality and rarely need service.

Besides competitive advantage, a firm must choose its competitive scope, either targeting a broad market or a narrow—or niche—market. A broad market scope implies that the firm targets the mass market or many market segments, whereas the narrow market scope focuses on one particular buyer group.

Combining the two types of competitive advantage with the two types of target markets results in four potential variations of generic strategy options. When the lower cost and differentiation strategies of a broad mass-market target are pursued, they are referred to as *cost leadership* and *differentiation*. When they are targeting only one buyer group, they are called *focus cost leadership* and *focus differentiation*.

According to Porter, the greatest danger in pursuing a generic strategy is the possibility of being stuck in the middle. From a competitive advantage standpoint, this occurs when a firm is unwilling to commit marketing and research-and-development resources needed to create a product or service that is perceived to be unique, or when a firm tries to keep costs low but does not aggressively pursue strategies that have the lowest cost in the industry. Regarding competitive scope, a firm that is pursuing a focus strategy can be stuck in the middle when it becomes overconfident and starts to go after many market segments or expand into the mass market without committing the necessary resources to successfully reach the larger market.

> A manufacturer should and must excel all competition in some way . . . the product can be more efficiently made and be cheaper in price . . . or designed for different uses. Or it may be applied to the customer's needs in a way that will make it more useful because of the application.
>
> —*James F. Lincoln*

Although Porter argues that achieving both a low-cost and a high-differentiation position is often temporary and cannot be sustained over the long term, some strategy scholars suggest that a "best cost" position is, in fact, achievable. The objective of the best-cost position is to deliver superior value to buyers by meeting expectations on key quality, service, or other features and having low enough costs to price the product lower than competitors. To become a best-cost provider, a company must have the resources and capabilities to achieve differentiation at a lower cost than rivals. For example, investments in technology allow firms to lower their costs while also improving performance in areas that differentiate the products or services. Wal-Mart's costs are the lowest in the industry, due to its technologically advanced distribution system that ensures efficient delivery of products and, at the same time, differentiates the company's services in the eyes of the consumers by having complete product assortment and availability.

While the best-cost position is an option for any firm, this strategy has risks for a company with a focus-market scope because it is hard to achieve both low-cost and meaningful differentiation when volume levels are low. Also, as Porter cautioned, any firm pursuing the best-cost position may get squeezed between the strategy of low-cost leaders, who are able to siphon customers away with the appeal of a lower cost, and high-end differentiators, who appeal to consumers with better product characteristics, service, or quality.

Exercise 1

Choosing How to Compete in the Lodging Industry

INSTRUCTIONS

Read the lodging industry profile in Part IV (pp. 137–140). On an individual basis, identify features and descriptive characteristics for five hypothetical companies in Table 8.1 on the following page. The information from the lodging industry profile provides background information about the industry and environmental trends.

TABLE 8.1 IDENTIFYING THE CHARACTERISTICS OF THE FOUR KINDS OF GENERIC STRATEGY

Strategy	Company Features and Description	Target Market	Environmental Trends That Support Strategy	Environmental Trends That Threaten Strategy
Cost leadership: Company A				
Differentiator: Company B				
Focus cost leadership: Company C				
Focus differentiator: Company D				
Stuck in the middle or best cost: Company E				

Adapted from Anisya Thomas. 1999. Introducing Students to business policy and strategy: Two exercises to increase participation and interest. *Journal of Management Education 23(4)*: 428–437. Used with permission.

Team Activity
Top Management Team

You are the top management team who is proposing a new hotel entering the lodging industry. You will be assigned Company A, B, C, D, or E by your instructor. Prepare a poster depicting the type of hotel you will build using the guidelines below and be sure to follow the strategy that has been assigned to your company. The poster will be used to sell the idea of the hotel and the organization to potential investors who might want to fund the company as it attempts to capture its target market. When you are finished, put your poster on the wall and choose one member of your group to "sell" your hotel and your organization. You have 45 minutes to complete this exercise.

Be prepared to discuss how your strategy will take advantage of environmental trends.

Guidelines for Preparing the Team Poster and Presentation

1. What kind of hotel would you build? What would it be called? Describe its five main features.

2. How would you market your hotel? To whom?

3. Describe three specific skills or resources you would use. How would you use them?

4. Describe two features of the organization (structure, incentive systems, etc.).

Exercise 2: Video
The Generic Strategy of Fossil, Inc.

INSTRUCTIONS

View the video about Fossil, Inc. The company is prospering despite the fact that cellphones and iPods have replaced wrist watches for many groups of consumers. The company no longer targets teens and instead develops fashion items for the 25 to 35-year-old consumer. Its watches range from $6 to $3,000 and are sold in Sears, JCPenney, Macy's, Nordstrom, and Neiman-Marcus. The company's products are also sold in company-owned Fossil stores and online directly from the firm. In order to identify Fossil's strategy, complete the chart below and then briefly discuss the generic strategy that the company follows.

1. List company features that support differentiation:	2. List company features that support cost leadership:

Who is the target market?

1. Based on the information about Fossil, what is the company's generic strategy? Briefly discuss.

_____

_____

Strategy Session 9
Build Your Competitive Advantage

> **O B J E C T I V E**
> In this session, you will learn to build competitive advantage through differentiation strategies.

To build competitive advantage, the firm begins by clarifying the marketplace in which it competes. This requires defining the customer need, who will be served, and how the need will be satisfied. When these questions are answered, the firm can then begin to seek to differentiate itself from its competitors.

To be successful in the marketplace, management identifies a generic strategy, which would dictate a set of consistent actions that the firm can undertake to build advantage over its rivals. As we outlined in Strategy Session 8, one viewpoint suggests that there are two broad categories of generic strategies: cost leadership and differentiation.

> We need to stand out from the crowd. Ads showing beautiful people dancing on beaches tell you nothing about the product or the brand.
>
> —*Andrew Morley, VP, Motorola*

However, a different framework was developed by Henry Mintzberg, a strategy scholar. He argued that cost leadership, as a generic strategy, does not directly lead to competitive advantage unless it is used to underprice rivals and thereby attract customers. The firm would not pursue a cost leadership strategy only to charge the same price as its rivals; the firm is really differentiating on the basis of price. Thus, Mintzberg claimed that cost leadership was just another form of differentiation.

Broadening this view and introducing more fine-grained choices, Mintzberg argued that the firm, in pursuit of competitive advantage, seeks to differentiate its products (which we will mean to include services) in six major ways. These are:

Differentiation by Price: In pursuing a lower price, the firm may be driven to follow a functional strategy that brings down costs, lowers quality, provides less service, offers fewer options, and so on. Everything else remaining the same, customers always prefer a lower price.

Differentiation by Image: To create an image is to create a psychological distinction where it does not otherwise exist, through careful marketing. In a sense, this is an artificial form of differentiation, since it is achieved by creating a different perception. For instance, since blind taste tests reveal that customers often cannot distinguish between different brands of beer, manufacturers work hard to build an image for their brand.

Differentiation by Support: Support refers to related products or services that go with the primary product. It may be included with the product or sold separately. Thus, it is a peripheral form of differentiation, such as the local pharmacy offering a 24-hour delivery service, or Mercedes-Benz offering free oil changes for the car for the first five years.

Differentiation by Quality: The effort here is to make the product itself better and not just different. Thus, the product does everything that competing products do; however, it does these things better through improved performance, or through its durability or reliability. Toyota's automobiles, for instance, are known to have fewer defects.

Differentiation by Design: The focus here is to offer something that is very different and to provide unique features. Apple's iPhone takes the lead over all its rivals with its special features. Sometimes, the uniqueness may be less ambitious, such as a fashion-conscious individual being attracted to a pair of "designer" jeans.

Undifferentiation: When the firm has no clear basis for differentiation, except perhaps through scope, it is following a policy of undifferentiation. The corner grocery store, in many cities, survives primarily based on its location, not because the owners offer anything special compared to the store a few blocks down the street. Firms that merely try to copy the actions of a main rival are also following undifferentiation.

These forms of differentiation need not be mutually exclusive. Some firms may try to combine different forms of differentiation to stand out in the marketplace. For example, IKEA, the furniture chain store, uses unique designs with a policy of the customer assembling the product so as to offer a lower price.

The firm has to choose the functional strategies it would follow to achieve the desired differentiation. When a cost-reduction strategy is followed all along the value chain, including sourcing cheaper components, etc., the firm can support a price differentiation strategy. Highly skilled advertising and promotion, within the function of marketing, perhaps with higher pricing, would be required to follow an image differentiation strategy. Competence in the areas of product development and care in manufacturing would be required to deliver on a quality differentiation strategy.

When the market space is sliced based on factors such as geography (mass market versus local market), how the customer buys (in the store or through the Internet), and so on, there are many segments to manage. When such segmentation is combined with the forms of differentiation described above, several possibilities exist to generate competitive advantage.

Exercise
Build Your Intended Strategy

INSTRUCTIONS
Read the case "Caffeine Satisfaction: Rivalry Among the Coffee Shops"
(pp. 145–150) before you come to class. Think about the industry, and study the
different strategies followed by the companies described in the case.

In class, as a team, you will assume the role of the top management of a particular coffee shop/chain. You now have the opportunity to set the strategy for the future. Your task is to discuss and formulate the intended strategy of your firm for the next five years based on your analysis of the competitive conditions in the market and your understanding of the firm and its capabilities.

Your team has 100 points. You may choose to acquire specific competencies listed in Table 9.1 that will form the basis of your strategy. Each method has a point allocation, and the total may not exceed 100. Write a paragraph describing your strategy by explaining how the competencies you have acquired will be used. Make a brief presentation to the class. Then await further instructions.

TABLE 9.1 COMPETITIVE METHODS

No.	Competitive Method	Points
1	Broad product range	25
2	Building brand identification	20
3	Capability to manufacture specialty products	20
4	Competitive pricing	25
5	Continuing overriding concern for cost reduction	15
6	Efficient logistics	15
7	Efforts to build reputation	15
8	Efforts to enhance quality of advertising	20
9	Efforts to insure availability of raw materials	25
10	Enforcing strict product quality control procedures	25
11	Extensive customer service capabilities	25
12	Forecasting market growth	15
13	Increased speed to market	15
14	Influencing channels of distribution	20
15	Information management	15

(continued)

TABLE 9.1   COMPETITIVE METHODS (continued)

No.	Competitive Method	Points
16	Innovation in manufacturing process	20
17	Innovations in marketing techniques and methods	25
18	Integrate vertically (backward/forward)	15
19	Maintaining low inventory levels	15
20	Maximize capacity utilization	15
21	New product development/innovation	25
22	Operating efficiency of business unit	20
23	Premium pricing	15
24	Products in high-price segments	20
25	Promotion and advertising above industry average	25
26	Protect technology through patents	15
27	Prudent management of receivables	15
28	Pursue scale economies	15
29	Quality of product	25
30	Reducing variety of products and channels	15
31	Refining existing products	15
32	Serving discriminating customers	15
33	Serving special geographic segments	20
34	Specific attempts to insure a pool of highly trained experienced personnel	20
35	Use of alliances	15

Strategy Session 10

Viewing Corporate Strategy from the Core Competencies Perspective

> OBJECTIVE
>
> In this session, practice designing corporate strategy for a diversified company from a core competencies perspective.

Corporate strategy deals with making choices about the direction for a firm as a whole and about the areas in which a company should compete. In choosing business areas, management decides whether to concentrate resources and create competitive advantage in one line of business or in one industry, such as McDonald's in the fast-food industry and Southwest Airlines in the airline industry, or to select and manage a mix of businesses competing in several industries, such as General Electric and Johnson & Johnson. Either way, issues of growth or downsizing become part of what is considered corporate-level strategic decision making.

> Core competencies are different for every organization; they are, so to speak, part of an organization's personality.
>
> —*Peter Drucker*

An earlier approach to corporate strategies of growth was by expanding product offerings and diversifying into different business areas. To help executives make decisions about how to divide organizational resources and where to invest new capital, several portfolio models were created. Among the most well known were the BCG growth/share matrix, the GE/McKinsey industry attractiveness and business strength model, and the Arthur D. Little matrix that incorporated life-cycle stages into the analysis. These techniques provided a convenient means for management to review the competitive position of diversified business units against one another all on one chart.

While these models simplified large amounts of information about a multidivisional firm's many holdings, the "portfolio of businesses" approach had limitations. It focused on viewing businesses in the portfolio as freestanding units, an approach that could fragment and misguide resource allocation. For example, pulling resources from a strong business unit that operated in a low-growth mature industry to fund an up-and-coming unit in a high-growth industry could actually result in the premature decline of the strong unit. Also, this approach gave little guidance to management in terms of what new businesses should be added to the company's holdings and how to increase overall revenues.

To promote a wider view of the firm beyond a collection of individual business units, Hamel and Prahalad created a framework that considers the firm as a portfolio of core competencies. The idea of core competencies in business comes from the resource-based view of strategic thinking. This view holds that strategy should be developed based on a company's unique resources and capabilities. Resources include capital equipment, the skills of employees, patents, finance, and talented managers. Capabilities are the skills needed to take full advantage of a firm's assets. Competitive advantage occurs when resources and capabilities are

- Valuable to a company's chosen direction
- Rare
- Costly to imitate
- Cannot easily be substituted

FIGURE 10.1 CORE COMPETENCIES

Resources and Capabilities

that are valuable, rare, costly to imitate,
nonsubstitutable

Core Competencies

When these four criteria are met, resources and capabilities become core competencies (see Figure 10.1).

By viewing the firm as a portfolio of core competencies rather than as a collection of individual business units, management is in a better position to identify acquisition and deployment goals. That is, it focuses attention on how a company can create value by building new competencies or by recombining existing competencies to enter new business areas.

To actively manage core competencies, managers must share a view of what those core competencies are. While many managers can articulate what is done well in the organization, it may be more difficult for them to separate competencies from the products or services offered. For example, at Canon, the core competencies are not its color copiers or bubble jet printers, but rather its capability for precision mechanics, fine optics, and electronic imaging that result in the end products. Therefore, the first step in creating this type of portfolio is to identify an inventory of competencies separate from the inventory of products or services.

The matrix below shows these two dimensions (core competencies and products) at two time frames: existing and new. The inventory discussed above of existing competencies and existing products falls in the lower left quadrant of the matrix. Once the inventory is prepared, management is ready to move to the next step of considering strategic options. Are there opportunities to strengthen the company's position in a particular product area by importing competencies that may exist elsewhere in the company? This was a strategy adopted by General Electric when it transferred competencies between its power generator business and its jet engine business, both of which rely on advanced materials and engineering skills to produce large turbines.

Other strategic options involve considering new core competencies and new products (see Figure 10.2). The advantage of this framework is that it seeks to identify and exploit the interlinkages across units. Whether management chooses to diversify into related or unrelated industries or whether the company remains in one industry and competencies are shared across product lines, this technique keeps management focused on adding value to the corporate whole from a resource-based, core competencies perspective.

FIGURE 10.2 NEW CORE COMPETENCIES AND NEW PRODUCTS

Core Competencies	New	What new core competencies are needed to protect and extend existing markets?	What new core competencies would we need to participate in new markets?
	Existing	This is the existing portfolio or inventory of competencies and products. What is the opportunity to improve the company's position in existing markets through existing core competencies?	What new products or services could be created through recombining current core competencies?
		Existing	New
		Products	

Exercise

Corporate Strategy at Honda

INSTRUCTIONS
Read and use the Honda profile below to complete Table 10.2 as part of a team activity. The table appears at the end of the exercise.

Honda Motor Company Limited

In 1946, Honda Technical Research Institute, a manufacturer of motors for motorized bicycles, became the Honda Motor Company. By the 1950s, the newly formed Honda Motor Company became one of the leading motorcycle manufacturers in the world, and in 1963 the firm launched its first sports car in Japan. By 1967 the company was producing automobiles in its Suzuka factory, and it established a manufacturing plant in the United States in 1980. Its expertise in small engines and power trains led to other products such as power units, generators, lawn mowers, tillers, snow throwers, water pumps, marine engines, and electric wheelchairs.

The research and development (R&D) center of Honda was set up as an independent subsidiary in 1960 and is considered one of the secrets to the company's success. Unlike Toyota, which is considered to be more structured and bureaucratic, Honda is entrepreneurial. Employee satisfaction and loyalty are strong in the R&D center due to the high value placed on creativity and independence. Located in Saitama, west of Tokyo, the engineers in this subsidiary create every product that the company makes and pursues new projects on the side. Although the subsidiary reports to Honda Motor Company, it is recognized throughout the company as a very influential and powerful group. In fact, every CEO has come from the R&D Center. The current CEO, Takeo Fukui, spent 20 years working on motorcycles in R&D. He meets only once or twice each year with the R&D employees, and he prefers to give them as much freedom as possible without oversight from him.

In 1986 one team in the R&D group began research into aviation. Although Honda decided to move the team to another project, the group persisted in working on the aviation project on the side. This tinkering continued, and in 1997 a new design for a plane with the engines mounted above the wings was presented to management. The roomier cabin and greater fuel economy which resulted from the new configuration won over management, and the project was at the forefront again. What became known as the Hondajet made its first flight in 2003, and the company started taking orders in 2006. In late August of 2006, Honda set up a wholly owned subsidiary, Honda Aircraft Company, which is responsible for further development, sales promotion, and production of the Hondajet. Based in Greensboro, North Carolina, near the Piedmont Triad International Airport, the very light passenger jet is due to go on sale in 2010 for $3.9 million. The company has orders for 100 planes and expects to sell 70 per year.

Another innovation from the group is a humanoid robot called ASIMO (advanced step in innovative mobility). It speaks, balances on one foot (34 small electric motors are required to accomplish this movement), is able to kick a soccer ball, recognize faces, and distinguishes sounds. First displayed at Expo 2005 in Japan, the robot resembles a small astronaut wearing a backpack and is able to walk similarly to humans at a speed of 3.7 mph. It is the world's only humanoid that can go up and down stairs independently. Plans for displaying the robot are part of a 10-year business alliance with Disneyland. Honda will sponsor the theme park's anniversary festivities and will exhibit the ASIMO robot.

The company has three new electric hybrid vehicles in the works, and in June 2008 it produced the first assembly-line hydrogen-powered fuel-cell vehicle. More efficient than a hybrid, its FCX Clarity car combines hydrogen and oxygen from ordinary air to make electricity. There are no pollutants and the only byproducts are heat and water. The car does not require a rechargeable battery nor does it use electricity, and the company is developing a hydrogen home-refueling station that takes up the space of a refrigerator.

Net sales for the company's four business segments (automobile, motorcycle, financial services, and power products/other business) totaled 12,002.8 billion yen in 2008 as compared to 11,087.1 billion yen in 2007. Net income rose to 600 billion yen in 2008 from 592.3 billion yen in 2007. Unit sales for the company's manufactured-product business segments is shown in Table 10.1.

TABLE 10.1 UNITS SOLD (THOUSANDS) BY THE COMPANY'S MANUFACTURED PRODUCT BUSINESS SEGMENTS*

Business Segment	2004	2005	2006	2007	2008
Automobile business	2,983	3,242	3,391	3,652	3,925
Motorcycle business	9,206	10,482	10,271	10,369	9,320
Power product business	5,047	5,300	5,876	6,421	6,057
Total	17,236	19,024	19,538	20,442	19,302

*Figures are for Financial Year ending 31 March.

Rating the Honda Company

Name(s): _____

1. Complete the information for Honda in the boxes in Table 10.2. Next to each product, give a rating that identifies whether the product is linked to the core competencies (5 = closely linked; 3 = somewhat linked; 1 = very limited linkage).

2. Once you have completed Table 10.2, using the scale below, rate how well you think the company overall has linked its core competencies to its products:

   Rating = _____

   5 = Linkage is the strongest that it has been in the company's history.

   4 = Linkage is improving as a result of new products.

   3 = Linkage is the same now as it was when the company started.

   2 = Link is getting weaker as a result of new products.

   1 = No linkage between core competencies and products exists.

3. Briefly note opportunities that may exist for the company to further leverage its core competencies and what issues may be of concern for this diversified firm.

TABLE 10.2

Core Competencies	Products

Strategy Session 11
Global Strategic Alliances

OBJECTIVE

In this session, the goal is to understand the objectives and nature of cooperation between companies in a strategic alliance, and the decisions required to make an alliance work. Following this introductory reading, review and reconsider the General Motors–Toyota strategic alliance.

A strategic alliance may be defined very broadly as any arrangement or agreement under which two or more firms cooperate to achieve certain commercial objectives. Given this definition, the term covers a wide range of options, from simple agreements to buy and sell each other's goods, to creating separate and legally distinct ventures. Although the objectives of an alliance can vary widely, if properly dealt with, an alliance can be a relatively inexpensive way of achieving targeted objectives.

Cooperation faces us in the business world in several ways. It may occur within the framework of a contract, or not. In Strategy Session 6 we came across the role of the complementor, a player who causes a customer to value your product more. In the personal computer industry, for example, Hewlett-Packard and Dell are competitors, but they are complementors to Intel, the maker of computer processor chips, and Microsoft, the maker of computer operating system software. Cooperation between Microsoft and Intel and Hewlett-Packard benefits technological improvements and overall growth of the market.

Game theory and transaction cost analysis are two ways of explaining why firms might consider creating a strategic alliance within a contractual framework. Game theory suggests that firms cooperate rather than compete when benefits are maximized—so the alliance can be seen as an example of how cooperation can maximize benefits for the two partners. However, the nature of an alliance, especially when it involves two players in the same or related industry, suffers from some inherent contradictions. The contradictions occur because there are positive and defensive objectives associated with the alliance, even though the two partners will not enter into an alliance unless they hope to gain more from cooperating than being on their own.

On the positive side, the objectives for each partner are to add value to the activity on which they are cooperating and to enhance their competencies through learning from the partner. On the defensive side, the objective is to avoid becoming too dependent on the partner (which can reduce the firm's flexibility in strategic decision making), and to avoid its core competencies being absorbed and learned by the partner. The latter situation, in particular, may make that firm less attractive and reduce its competitive edge.

These conflicting objectives can cause tension and lead to failure. Thus, there is a need for careful structuring of the alliance. Before entering into an agreement, the parties must carefully select each other, be clear about their objectives, bring complementary strengths to the alliance, and ensure the benefits to cooperation are maximized. Sometimes entering into long-term commitments can help achieve these benefits.

> In the fluid global marketplace, it is no longer possible or desirable for single organizations to be entirely self-sufficient. Collaboration is the value of the future. Alliances are the structure of the future.
>
> —Joel Bleeke and David Ernst

Transaction cost analysis theory explains that ownership of resources is more efficient than contracting for goods and services when the transaction cost of buying goods on the open market becomes too great. Thus, an alliance should deliver greater benefits to the two parties than what might be achieved from a purely market-based transaction between them or with others for similar goods and services. That is, if the two parties can achieve their objectives through outsourcing their needs, or outright purchase of components, there is no need to enter into an alliance. As a result, this approach calls for detailed contractual agreements between the parties that clearly cover the cost-benefit issues; and as trust develops, the costs can be reduced with less supervision and better interaction between the partners.

Whether an alliance is created because cooperation offers greater benefits or because transaction costs can be reduced, parties go through three important stages. These are (1) the careful selection of a partner, (2) negotiation and structuring of the agreement, and (3) the post-agreement management of the alliance. Other factors that contribute to a successful alliance are:

1. The partnership should preferably be between "equals." When partners bring complementary skills and keep their objectives clear, there is less room for confusion.

2. An ownership interest and clearly stated contractual rights and obligations help cement and deepen commitment to the alliance.

3. Partners should recognize differences in management styles and cultures and work toward dealing with these issues openly and in a sensitive manner.

4. Regular review of progress in the alliance keeps a focus on objectives and prevents problems from getting too large before they are sorted out.

Exercise

Renewing the General Motors–Toyota Alliance

INSTRUCTIONS

Read the case below and complete the first question in the form that follows, before coming to class. Then, in class, the instructor will have you form teams and provide you with updated information and instructions for the next step of this exercise.

NUMMI: The GM–Toyota Alliance

In 1983, General Motors (GM) and Toyota entered into an alliance that resulted in the creation of the New United Motor Manufacturing Incorporated (NUMMI, www.nummi.com), a new company to be equally owned by the two parents and with equal representation on the board of directors. Toyota's contribution to NUMMI was $100 million in cash. GM also contributed the same amount, made up of $20 million in cash and its plant in Fremont, California, which would be the NUMMI manufacturing facility. GM's plant had been idle for a year. Started in 1963, it had been shut down and its workers laid off due to poor labor–management relations, high absenteeism, and the alcohol-related problems of employees, which had affected operations.

Japanese automotive companies had been under some pressure from their government to alleviate the trade friction between the U.S. and Japan by commencing manufacturing in the U.S. Honda and Nissan had initiated plants in the U.S. Toyota had intentions of being in the North American market for the long term, but was not sure how it would deal with the United Auto Workers (UAW), the labor union in the auto industry, and with U.S. suppliers. The company hoped that an alliance with GM would help it learn how to work with these groups, understand the complexity of logistics in the vast country, and achieve its global strategy of a manufacturing presence in the United States. GM had two objectives for its alliance with Toyota. One was to gain quick access to a world-class small car, a gap in GM's product line that could be filled by Toyota's strengths in this area. The other was to utilize an idle plant. Moreover, the alliance would also allow GM to learn about Toyota's famous production system (TPS). This system was credited with having achieved very low inventory levels and high efficiency.

Under the terms of the alliance, Toyota appointed NUMMI's top officers, including the CEO and president. GM assigned up to 16 executives three-year assignments on a rotating basis. NUMMI would be a stamping and assembly operation, and components would be supplied both from Japan (by Toyota) and other suppliers in the United States. Toyota agreed to GM's condition that the laid-off UAW workers would be employed in the plant. In negotiations with UAW—which it undertook on its own—Toyota achieved the flexibility it wanted in working conditions and job assignments, such as having only three job classifications for the workers. The plant previously had over one hundred.

In managing NUMMI, Toyota followed many of its established practices. Initially many workers were sent to Japan for training. It carefully selected employees, trained workers for more than one job, and delegated decision making to small worker teams.

Executive dining rooms were given up for a common cafeteria, managers wore the same uniforms as the workers, and there were no reserved parking spaces for executives.

The plant maintained high quality and productivity standards. The production rate achieved was about 60 cars per hour using only about one-third of the workers in a comparable auto plant elsewhere. Press reports quoted workers' representatives who complained about the fast pace, yet they participated in ongoing learning and continuous improvement. The company was credited with having established a problem-solving approach in its relationship with the same union that formerly fought GM's management. Under Toyota's management, absenteeism dropped from 22% to 2%. J.D. Power and Associates ranked NUMMI as one of the best auto plants on initial quality in 2002.

NUMMI employed about 5,400 workers and could manufacture up to 400,000 cars. There were plans to invest in additional production lines. The plant produced *Tacoma* pickup trucks and *Corolla* sedans for Toyota and the Pontiac *Vibe* for GM. The *Vibe* (identical to the Toyota *Matrix*) was developed jointly with GM providing the styling and Toyota undertaking the design and engineering. Although NUMMI produces cars for both GM and Toyota, marketing is the responsibility of the respective parent.

From the start, thousands of GM employees took tours of the facility. In 1985, GM created a Technical Liaison Office in Fremont to document the learning and disseminate it through GM. However, while individual managers learned the TPS during their tour of duty, there was little effort in transferring the knowledge to the organization. There was also resistance within the GM organization to importing these methods. However, in 1992, Jack Smith, who had headed the GM negotiating team, became chairman and made the learning from NUMMI a priority issue. Slowly, the TPS began to be implemented successfully in several GM plants around the world. GM executives attributed the increase in quality of their cars to the learning from Toyota. Three GM plants were ranked among the best in quality in North America and tied with the NUMMI plant. GM also learned how to build small cars properly and build flexibility in duties among line workers. The close working relationship also gave GM an insight into Toyota's organization and operating systems. However, aspects of Toyota's proprietary engineering and manufacturing processes that were outside the partnership were not accessible to GM.

Toyota moved fast in its expansion in North America. Within a year of commencing operations at NUMMI, Toyota began planning its first assembly plant, which was established in Georgetown, Kentucky. The company learned how to deal with local suppliers and sourced from over 500 suppliers in North America. By 2008, Toyota had eight manufacturing/assembly plants in North America, and produced about two-thirds of the vehicles it sold there.

Alumni of NUMMI went on to head important positions in both companies. When Toyota needed a manager with experience in pickup truck production for its *Tundra* pickup plant, it hired Mr. Norm Bafunno, a GM production manager who had spent time at NUMMI. Toyota was looking to break into the pickup market dominated by the three U.S. automakers.

Collaborations notwithstanding, GM and Toyota exhibited normal competitive behavior. GM's share of the U.S. market fell from 44.6% in 1980 to 28.4% in 2002, while Toyota's share grew from 6.4% to 10.4% over the same period. By 2007, Toyota's share was 16%; GM's was 24%. GM was beset not only by falling market share, but also shrinking profitability due to its high cost of operations. It was following a strategy of cutting capacity and forgoing low profit sales (and thereby market share) in order to get back to profitability. It entered into a landmark agreement with the UAW to transfer healthcare and pension liability to the union for its retired workers, which had resulted in an inflated cost structure.

Toyota's chairman, Hiroshi Okuda, had set a goal of reaching a 15% global market share by 2010 (up from about 12% in 2005). However, he was also concerned with the potential negative perception that Toyota's rising market share would create in the U.S. where the domestic automobile companies occupied a special place in the psyche of the population. Thus, Toyota spread its vehicle, engine, and parts factories through eight states in the U.S., sprinkling manufacturing jobs and building a network of favorably inclined state and federal politicians. In 2005, Okuda told reporters in Tokyo, "I am very much concerned about GM's plight. I am concerned not just about GM but the state of America's entire auto industry as a whole." He indicated that Toyota would share technology with U.S. car makers and even raise prices to give them "breathing room."

Toyota's production system, also called "lean manufacturing," was more than *kanban* (where parts arrive just in time for manufacture) and a method in which productivity and quality were maintained at high levels. It was a broad system that engaged its participants in their work with an ideology that appealed to their hearts and minds. As Haruo Shimada of Japan's Keio University said, the Toyota system amounts to "humanware," combining management, participation, incentives, and technology to optimize productivity, motivation, and the development of people at work. Mr. Bafunno commented that although the famed TPS was not unique anymore, since many manufacturers had adopted it in their own factories, he saw several differences in the way Toyota ran its production. The rules focused on the factory workers, giving them the power to make improvements in production, eliminate waste, and make quality judgments about the product, practices that he did not see elsewhere.

Toyota's new manufacturing technology, called "simple and slim," was installed in its San Antonio plant. The technology used smaller, lighter machinery, and reduced plant size by one-third of a comparable GM plant. Toyota also developed a shorter assembly line in Japan that could churn out different cars simultaneously on the same line every 50 seconds. It has not yet been introduced in the U.S.

Due to concerns about global warming, auto companies were under pressure to lower the average fuel consumption of their vehicles. In 2004, California passed a law requiring a 30% reduction in global-warming emissions from cars and light trucks by 2016. Other states in the U.S. were expected to follow. Hybrids were expected to account for 8% of total U.S. auto sales by 2012. Toyota pioneered this product with its *Prius* and shared the technology with Ford and Nissan. GM rejected the nickel-metal hydride battery on which the Prius was based; its present hybrid models are only a slight improvement over gas engines. Both companies were working independently on lithium-ion batteries which are lighter and more powerful.

Based on your reading of the case, complete the question below.

1. What are the areas of cooperation and conflict that arise from the NUMMI alliance for both companies? Use Table 11.1 to answer this question. Try to separate the issues you would consider strategic and operational for the organization.

TABLE 11.1 AREAS OF COOPERATION AND CONFLICT

	Cooperation	Conflict
Strategic		
Operational		

Team Activity
Negotiations

After negotiation of the NUMMI contract in class, answer the following questions. Check your team's "company" as appropriate:

☐ Toyota   ☐ GM

1. What objectives did you have in mind for the negotiation?

_____

_____

_____

_____

_____

2. What elements in the new agreement help in maximizing the benefit for your company?

_____

_____

_____

_____

_____

3. What elements in the agreement have minimized the potential for future conflicts?

_____

_____

_____

_____

_____

4. How would you judge whether NUMMI is a success or not?

_____

_____

_____

_____

_____

Strategy Session 12
Identifying Transnational Strategies

O B J E C T I V E

This session develops an understanding of global, multidomestic, and transnational strategies. The exercise leads you through the decisions that would be taken in two global footwear giants, Bata Shoes and Nike, as they execute their strategies.

Due to the trend toward globalization of most sectors of the economy, more organizations today have strategies that involve them in business operations worldwide. As companies ponder the strategy they should adopt in different nations, they are faced with the choice of following a common strategy across all nations or designing a unique one for each country. Should operations and products be standardized or customized? This choice is commonly referred to in the literature as "global versus multidomestic strategy."

A company following a *global strategy* tends to take a centralized and coordinated view of its strategy across the globe since it believes that the similarities of markets allow for exploiting a common strategy. These companies are highly focused on global profitability and would therefore coordinate activities across the world to maximize the benefits derived from each location and operation. The marketing, R&D, production, and other operational activities of this company may be distributed across the globe or concentrated in one place depending on scale/scope economies and how it fits a global plan. These companies tend to have rather standardized products and thus cater to a customer segment that has generic attributes across countries and is not seeking local responsiveness. This approach is on the rise, as products with worldwide acceptance continue to emerge and as less expensive transportation and communication networks make globalization efficient and effective. One disadvantage of this strategy is that companies may not be able to market to segments that may be looking for something different.

A company that follows a *multidomestic strategy* tends to look upon its strategy in each country as being independent of that in another, since it believes that national markets differ significantly in their structure and key success factors. This strategy gives a high preference to location and national considerations. In each individual country, operations would tend to be involved in as many value creation activities as possible, including marketing, production, financing, R&D, and other operational activities. Three social forces encourage customized operations and products. First, cultural differences continue to exist among countries, and different tactics are necessary to target these differences. Second, governments often require that organizations follow legal mandates of the host nation. Third, as competition increases, local firms become aggressive niche players that closely tailor their products and services to consumer needs. One disadvantage of this approach is that multinational organizations may not get the benefits of the experience-curve of the company as a whole as country operations run independent of each other.

A company that follows a *transnational strategy* seeks to achieve both global efficiency and local responsiveness. This is difficult to implement since it requires close

> Pernod's strategy is to be present in every single wine and spirits market through its local roots, global reach strategy.
>
> —*Pierre Pringuet, MD,*
> *Pernod Ricard SA*

global coordination and flexibility at the national level. Firms need to build sophisticated networks for integration across some business functions (say, sourcing materials), while at the same time delegating authority to local managers for other functions (say, marketing). Thus, it can be seen as falling in between global and multidomestic strategies. When effectively implemented, a transnational strategy can deliver higher performance than purely global or multidomestic strategies.

Figure 12.1 illustrates these choices on a continuum from standardized to customized strategy.

FIGURE 12.1   THE CONTINUUM BETWEEN GLOBAL AND MULTIDOMESTIC STRATEGIES

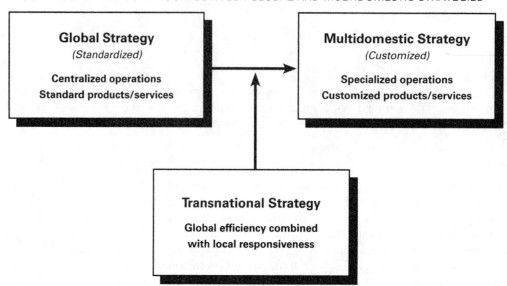

Exercise

Global Operations of Bata Shoe and Nike

INSTRUCTIONS
Read the company profiles of Bata and Nike. In questions 1–8 that follow, circle the appropriate response in the scale below each statement. Then write a brief response to question 9.

Bata Shoe Organization[1]

The Bata Shoe Organization (BSO) runs the global operations of Bata Ltd. Based in Lausanne, Switzerland, it is credited with being the world's largest manufacturer and retailer of footwear, selling about 140 million pairs a year. BSO has a reputation for manufacturing sturdy yet stylish mass-merchandized shoes—both formal and casual—for men, women, and children. (Being privately owned, financial performance figures are not released, but 2007 sales revenues are estimated at $3 billion.) It retails in 50 countries, employing about 40,000 people. It owns 5,000 stores, apart from distributing through several thousand franchisees worldwide. Its 40 operating units in 26 countries include shoe manufacturing, mold making, quality control laboratories, hosiery units, and tanneries. The operating companies are grouped into four regional business units that, according to BSO, are based on similarities in markets and business issues. Each unit benefits from synergies in product development, sourcing, and market appeal. The four business units include Bata Asia Pacific-Africa, based in Singapore; Bata Europe, based in Lausanne; Bata Latin America, based in Mexico City; and Bata North America, based in Toronto.

The Batas, a family of shoemakers, began operations in 1894 in Czechoslovakia, and had built a shoe network in 28 countries by the 1930s. Tom Bata Sr., the tenth generation, migrated to Canada at the time of the Nazi invasion of the country. In recent times, he, along with his son Thomas J. Bata, was largely responsible for building the company to its present status. In 2001, his grandson, Thomas G. Bata, was appointed chairman. Eighty-five percent of BSO's subsidiaries are wholly owned; although in some countries, due to local regulations, Bata Ltd. has only a minority ownership. Where it has no equity, it provides licensing, consulting, and technical assistance. BSO keeps a watchful eye over its autonomous subsidiaries. For instance, Bata India, the largest subsidiary in the Asia group, is 51% owned by Bata Ltd. and had a record loss of $9.8 million in 1995. BSO intervened by sending expatriate managers with turnaround experience and providing fresh investments and an interest-free loan of $10 million. The new managing director, Stephen Davies, moved from Bangladesh with a charge to focus on marketing. Similarly, problems in Uganda led to closing operations there with the market to be served from its production center in neighboring Kenya.

Factories and stores are built to standard specifications around the world. Bata focuses on low-cost manufacturing and builds a local network of retailers and suppliers

---

[1] For more information about Bata, visit its corporate Web site at http://www.bata.com.

around it. It takes advantage of local materials in the countries where its plants are based. It prefers to produce in a given market nearly everything it sells there.

The company operates in several developing countries and is conscious of its role as a provider of jobs in the economy. While top management may be composed of expatriates, local personnel are inducted, trained, and given increasing responsibilities. Regular training programs are conducted at headquarters for senior worldwide employees. Country-based training programs work toward solutions to local problems that are culturally sensitive to their area.

BSO deals with a variety of political environments and has units in democratic and totalitarian regimes. In some countries, its operations have been nationalized and then denationalized. It sponsors local sporting events and engages with the local communities, such as supporting Junior Achievement (an organization that promotes entrepreneurship) and AIDS education. Many of the company's factories are located away from urban centers. In some countries, Bata provides housing, schools, and other amenities for its workers. Tariff protection and other government incentives have helped protect its market in some places.

The arrival of manufacturers such as Nike and Adidas, however, into the industry on a global scale caused consumer preferences to change dramatically. Innovation and brand image in the footwear industry in the early 1990s forced the industry to be more market driven rather than manufacturing driven. From 1995 to 1996, Bata closed about 20% of its outlets—as many of them had begun to lose money—and the company restructured its operations in Europe. Bata's strategy is to provide footwear at affordable prices to the largest possible segment of the population, but in some African markets it has faced competition from Chinese imports and second-hand goods. It has also opened its own procurement center in China. More recently, in various markets around the world, it has begun to renovate its stores and revitalize its image from traditional and conservative to modern and up market and work toward a globally integrated marketing.

Nike Inc.[2]

Nike Inc., based in Beaverton, Oregon (U.S.), manufactures a wide variety of high-quality athletic footwear and other accessories. The company was founded in 1964 by Phil Knight, a long distance runner, who remains chairman, and his coach, Bill Bowerman. Their goal was to design lightweight running shoes. The company catalog lists **over** 800 models for use in about 25 different sports and leisure activities. The company has six divisions along categories of sports, with each division combining shoes and apparel: running, soccer, basketball, men's training, women's fitness, and sports culture (products for casual wear). In 2007, Nike posted revenues of $16.3 billion. It plans to reach global sales of $23 billion by 2011 by focusing on fast growing regions such as China, India, Russia, and Brazil.

The focus of the company is sports and fitness and it creates and markets its shoes, accessories, and related products to males and females between 18 and 34 years. Its success began with manufacturing running shoes for jogging, a popular activity in the United States. As it expanded, it successfully faced the challenge of bringing into its product line shoes popular in other regions, such as European-style soccer shoes, cricket shoes, and shoes for skateboarding. In each sports line, it targets its premium sports footwear at the high performance athlete while other models are designed and priced for the general consumer.

Nike's strategy is built around individual sports and star players. The company has used famous sports personalities such as Michael Jordan (basketball), Roger Federer (tennis), and Tiger Woods (golf) as celebrity spokespersons and "signs" them to lucrative endorsement contracts with the belief that consumers will purchase Nike shoes and remain loyal to a brand name that is so closely identified with successful athletes. It

---

[2] For more information about Nike, visit its corporate Web site at http://www.nike.com.

views Adidas as its global rival. Advertising, although centrally developed, is adapted to local cultures.

Nike sells its products from its online store, and also through its own stores, footwear chain stores (such as Foot Locker), department stores, and franchises in 200 countries. It very closely monitors its international marketing and consolidated distribution operations in 24 centers across the world for better control over marketing. The company's R&D centers in the U.S., Taiwan, and South Korea work on new technologies and advanced materials with which to update shoe models at least every six months.

The company has contracted with over 700 manufacturers in 52 mostly low-wage countries including China, Thailand, Vietnam, Indonesia, and the Philippines to produce its products. Company technicians work closely with these contract factories. The company's production system is closely tied to its order-booking program, in which retailers order up to six months in advance of delivery and receive discount rates. Quick delivery is also ensured, where necessary, through bypassing its distribution centers, and moving directly to retail.

In the early 90s Nike faced unwanted publicity about sweatshop conditions in some of its contract factories, and has since worked to resolve the issues through better supervision and setting a code of conduct. Nike's growth has also come from acquisitions of companies such as Converse (sports footwear), Umbro (soccer shoes and apparel), and Cole Haan (casual luxury footwear).

1. Each company perceives its target consumers as having similar needs across the globe.

   Bata: To a lesser extent 1 2 3 4 5 To a greater extent
   Nike: To a lesser extent 1 2 3 4 5 To a greater extent

2. The Chinese factory's union has raised a dispute about poor working conditions. This matter is to be reported to the headquarters.

   Bata: To a lesser extent 1 2 3 4 5 To a greater extent
   Nike: To a lesser extent 1 2 3 4 5 To a greater extent

3. The marketing manager wishes to launch a new promotional campaign. This is a matter to be discussed and approved at a senior level in the headquarters.

   Bata: Less likely 1 2 3 4 5 More likely
   Nike: Less likely 1 2 3 4 5 More likely

4. The plant manager wishes to hire more workers to meet production needs. She would need to obtain prior approval from the headquarters.

   Bata: Less likely 1 2 3 4 5 More likely
   Nike: Less likely 1 2 3 4 5 More likely

5. In this company, the production schedule for each plant would need to be closely coordinated with the sales plan on a global basis.

   Bata: To a lesser extent 1 2 3 4 5 To a greater extent
   Nike: To a lesser extent 1 2 3 4 5 To a greater extent

6. This company sees a need for better coordination among its offices for operational efficiencies. What would be the appropriate basis on which to undertake the restructuring?

   Bata: Geographic / By product lines
   Nike: Geographic / By product lines

7. A manager on a field visit has identified a new line of footwear for use in schools in their physical education classes. Would prior permission be needed from headquarters in order to proceed?

   Bata: Prior permission needed / Not needed
   Nike: Prior permission needed / Not needed

8. In light of the responses to the above, what strategy would you say the company is following globally?

Bata:	Global strategy	1	2	3	4	5	Multidomestic strategy
Nike:	Global strategy	1	2	3	4	5	Multidomestic strategy

9. Speculate on trends in the industry over the next 10 years with respect to (a) consumer preferences for footwear, (b) national investment policies, and (c) any other. What changes would you recommend the company initiate in its strategy/operations to best face these trends, and why?

Bata:

_____

_____

_____

_____

_____

_____

_____

Nike:

_____

_____

_____

_____

_____

_____

_____

_____

_____

_____

Strategy Session 13
Understanding Turnaround Management

OBJECTIVE

The purpose of this session is to help develop an understanding of the critical issues surrounding organizational decline and the nature of turnaround management. An understanding of these issues enables managers to better understand the consequences of inaction and assist in developing a viable turnaround strategy. The exercise provides an opportunity to use analytical skills to assess decline and turnaround.

Most management theories are built on the assumption of a firm seeking growth and profitability. Thus, when an organization is undergoing decline in its performance with the prospect of eventual failure, it faces an experience for which it has limited preparation. An understanding of the processes of decline and the principles of effective turnaround management are skills that prospective managers need to have to develop viable turnaround strategies.

How few there are who have courage enough to own their faults, or resolution enough to mend them!

—Benjamin Franklin,
Poor Richard's Almanac

Decline in performance is common in the workplace. Most organizations face occasional decline that is quickly reversed. The causes that lead to these drops in performance are external and internal to the organization. External causes include general economic recession, regulatory actions, changes in consumer buying practices, and competitive actions, for example. Internal causes deal with poor management and include a wide range of issues such as over expansion, an improper fit between the company and its environment, poor marketing or product problems, and lack of effective controls. When the managers take timely action in dealing with the causes and reverse the trend, it is a part of the normal management function. However, research has shown that this does not always happen. In the early stages of decline, managers may deny the severity of the problems, not identify the causes of the problem correctly, and thus the decline continues.

As the firm continues to decline, the severity of the problems worsens and the organization starts incurring cash losses. Other signs may include the exit of valuable personnel. The firm now enters a critical phase and usually it takes some kind of a crisis to shake the organization into realizing the severity of its problems. It could be termination of the CEO, or a bank refusing further credit terms to the organization. When this happens, the firm realizes the need for drastic actions to stem the decline. These actions would be targeted toward cutting costs by improving efficiencies and reducing wasteful expenditures. Employees may be laid off and activities shrunk. The organization may also have to resort to selling assets to raise necessary funds. Quite often at this stage, several members of the top management team may be replaced in order to bring in new skills for the turnaround.

When the decline has been stabilized (that is, when the cash loss has been stemmed), then revenue-generating measures may be instituted, such as increasing sales and new product developments. The firm is now on a turnaround path that should be directed toward building its competencies back.

The key principles of turnaround management are precise identification from a strategic perspective of the causes of the organization's decline and turnaround strategies that incorporate key stakeholders.

1. It is important to take care in *identifying the causes of the problems*. Since actions need to be taken to deal with the causes, the more precise the firm is in identifying the problems, the higher the probability of the turnaround effort succeeding. Turnaround management consists of careful review of the causes before actions to correct the problems are defined. Causes of the problems should be grouped into strategic and operational categories. Strategic causes will include: what businesses the firm is in, whether it has the skills to be in those businesses, and how it competes in those businesses. Operational causes will deal with functional areas and include problems in marketing (advertising and promotional issues), human resources (pay, training, etc.), production (plant size, equipment, etc.), and so on.

2. The key point is that *management must deal with the strategic causes*. If the firm does not have the skills to be successful in the business and is experiencing a poor fit with its environment, then it needs to change its direction, reexamine its niche, and perhaps alter the strategy it is following to compete in this business. No amount of operational efficiencies will help if it has not fixed its strategic problems.

3. To achieve a turnaround, the firm needs the *help and support of various stakeholders* such as vendors, distribution channels, customers, bankers, and the like. Part of the skill of implementing the turnaround lies in stakeholder management and the firm's ability to extract concessions from them in the short run. The right leadership is also a crucial factor in successful turnarounds.

Bankruptcy, as an option, is resorted to usually only under extreme circumstances. Under the U.S. Bankruptcy Code, firms usually choose one of two options. Under Chapter 7, the firm may opt for liquidation. Under Chapter 11, the firm may seek the protection from creditors while it implements a turnaround plan with the approval of the court. Firms resort to Chapter 11 filing only when they have exhausted all other options and need the protection that the court can give.

Exercise

The Decline–Turnaround Sequence

1. Define and review the extent of the decline:

_____

_____

_____

_____

2. What is the crisis? How was the decline recognized?

_____

_____

_____

_____

3. Complete the following table:

Cause of Decline:	**Turnaround Actions:**
External	*Strategic*
Internal	*Operational*
Stakeholders Involved:	**Their Role:**

4. Changes in the top management team (TMT):

_____

_____

_____

_____

5. Results: Has the decline been stemmed/turnaround achieved?

_____

_____

_____

_____

6. What actions do you recommend and why?

_____

_____

_____

_____

Strategy Session 14

Scenario Planning: Innovative Approaches for the Future

> OBJECTIVE
>
> Learn the process of constructing innovative scenarios as a means to aid strategic decision making while dealing with an uncertain future environment.

Strategic decision making involves managers making decisions in the present to strengthen the position of the firm in the future. Under reasonably stable environments, it may be possible to forecast the future by extrapolating the conditions of the past. However, in dynamic environments, where there are several variables at play, the past is not likely to repeat itself. Customer needs change, regulatory conditions vary, availability of inputs is constrained, and competitors may be sharpening their plans. Building scenarios is a way of dealing with an unknowable—that is, an uncertain—future in a systematic manner. It helps in several ways:

> Scenarios are stories about the way the world might turn out tomorrow, stories that can help us recognize and adapt to changing aspects of our environment.
>
> —*Peter Schwartz,*
> *The Art of the Long View*

- Scenario planning leads to innovative thinking about the future because managers "stretch their minds" to reflect, brainstorm, and consider a wide range of possibilities.

- Scenario planning helps prepare firms for the unexpected by educating managers about uncertainty. It teaches them to understand and challenge their own assumptions.

- Scenarios can be the starting point for developing a strategy for the organization.

- Scenarios serve as a testing ground for ongoing strategies.

Scenarios, however, are not predictions. They are a way for managers to visualize different futures based on the probability of occurrence of events and trends.

The technique of scenario planning has been practiced since the 1960s. The company most closely associated with the method is the oil multinational Royal Dutch/Shell Group, which credited scenario planning for its quick and effective response to the oil crisis of 1973.* Another adherent is Duke Energy Corporation in the United States, which developed three scenarios to gauge the impact of events such as varying rates of economic growth, the role of the Internet, and the extent of deregulation of the energy industry to obtain what it calls euphemistically a "wind tunnel" for testing strategy.

Scenarios are short narratives describing a future state of affairs. The future state is based on observable trends, the present knowledge of experts and built on causal relationships. Different probabilities are assigned to the different ways in which events can develop in the future. This makes it possible to construct different scenarios of future states with the same set of events and trends. As time progresses, reality is constantly matched against the scenarios leading to their evaluation and refinement. In 2008, faced

---

* For more information about Royal Dutch/Shell's strategic use of scenarios, visit http://www.shell.com/scenarios.

with growing petro-nationalism, Royal Dutch/Shell revised its scenarios to consider situations where governments would dominate oil resources, and where they work to address climate change. The scenarios also become a framework against which the strategy can be evaluated and, if necessary, the direction altered.

Scenario descriptions are drawn focused on a single issue of critical importance to the company and are developed with internal consistency. This focal issue is the starting point for the development of scenarios. For Royal Dutch/Shell, one example would be scenarios that seek to answer the question: "Is there life for our company after the world runs out of oil?" Another example, say for a manufacturer of formal attire, are scenarios that address the issue: "Should we launch a line of fashion clothing for teenagers?" In both examples, the collection of quantitative and qualitative (such as expert opinions) data and the identification of social, cultural, technological, economic, and other kinds of environmental trends would be determined by the focal issue.

The writing of the scenario is a critical and innovative part of the process. This is the stage where facts, opinions, and expectations are woven into a narrative and form a plausible story. Yet the story needs to be analytical and not merely descriptive; namely, the logical development of events in the story should be clearly linked through cause-and-effect relationships. Given the interactions among the key driving forces in any situation, it is possible for several scenarios to be written. However, experts argue for a limited number—three or four—because too many scenarios may compromise the focus managers need for decision making.

Creation and use of scenarios, the two phases of the scenario planning process, are closely intertwined. Some scholars recommend that a best, worst, and most probable scenario be developed. The problem with this approach is that managers quickly commit to the middle path—and this builds rigidities in their response. A more sophisticated approach is to write the scenarios in a manner such that no one scenario becomes clearly preferable and all are equally plausible. This better achieves the purpose of getting managers to break from "mindsets" and to think innovatively of different possibilities, that is, "outside of the box." It is not necessary to commit to a particular scenario and when the existence of the scenarios is known widely among the key decision makers, managers can compare the unfolding reality with these scenarios and judge how further events may turn out.

Exercise

Develop Some Scenarios

Step 1. Focal Issue Identification

Identify one strategic issue for the future of Innkeepers of America that will set a direction for the company and involve major resource allocation. (As example, for a U.S. microprocessor manufacturer, the issue could be, "Shall we set up the R&D center for new chip design in India?"). State the focal issue in the form of a question on the line below:

Focal Issue: _____

Step 2. Key Factors in the Industry and General Environment

In Table 14.1, list the key factors (i.e., events or trends) that would influence the success or failure of the focal issue under different categories into the future. First, look for factors dealing with the industry environment (see Strategy Session 6 on p. 37) that *have a bearing on the focal issue.* Then, look for factors in the general environment. These deal with the macroeconomic, social, political/governmental, and technological forces. What events (i.e., single observable incidents) or trends (i.e., forces that bring about change) can affect the decision in these areas? Some may be predetermined, such as demographics, and others may be highly variable and subjective, such as issues of style or preferences.

Approach this step as a brainstorming exercise. First, let each member of the team take turns suggesting a factor under one of the listed categories. Do not evaluate but merely note it down in the first column of the table under Factors. Identify two or three in each category.

Step 3. Identify Importance and Assign Probabilities

Revisit each factor, and in column 2, on a five-point scale, assign numbers from 1 (unimportant) to 5 (very important) to reflect the importance of the factor identified for the success of the focal issue. Then, in column 3, assign a probability ranging from 0 (will not happen) to 1 (certain to happen) to reflect the certainty that you would attach to its occurrence.

Step 4. Building the Scenarios

Once a set of the critical uncertainties have been identified in the table, the scenario writing can begin. The scenarios will differ due to factors you have identified that are high

TABLE 14.1　FACTORS AFFECTING THE FUTURE

Factors	Importance Scale 1 (unimportant) to 5 (very important)	Probability of Occurrence Scale 0 (will not happen) to 1 (will happen)
Customers		
(e.g., PC manufacturers are demanding lower cost chips)	5	1
Suppliers		
Competitors		
Complementors		
Macroeconomic		
Social		
Political/Governmental		
(e.g., U.S. government may levy tariffs on imports)	3	0.2
Technological		

in importance and are uncertain (i.e., probability ~0.5). Each scenario may be a couple of paragraphs long. This is a creative process similar to story writing. Each scenario follows a "logic" or plot that ties the various elements together. Three typical themes are:

- **Winners and losers.** In this logic, resources are scarce, trade-offs are frequent, and there is usually one dominant player in the market.

- **Challenge and responses.** This scenario exhibits a kind of cyclical nature to events in which challenges arise and are met; there is a spirit of cooperation and accommodation.

- **Evolution.** In this scenario, changes take place slowly, organizations adapt to the changes while learning and adjustment take place.

Step 5. Scenario Elaboration

Although the most important forces identified in step 3 determine the logic of the scenario, every key factor needs to have a place in it. At this stage, the scenarios are checked to see if they are consistent internally, and distinct from each other. Identify data points—or signposts—for each scenario that can be tracked to judge which particular scenario is unfolding.

Step 6. Implications

Examine the focal issue in relation to each scenario. Respond to the following questions:

1. Do one or more scenarios support the decision posed in the focal issue?

2. Can the decision be altered so it is supported by more than one scenario?

Strategy Session 15

Succeeding in Strategy Formulation and Implementation   101

Exercise: Diagnosing Problems at Hewlett-Packard   103

Strategy Session 16

Structuring to Support Strategy   107

Exercise: Designing Organizational Structures for Club Ed   110

Strategy Session 17

Strategy Implementation Using the 7-S Model   113

Exercise: Transition at PeopleSoft   115

Strategy Session 18

Corporate Sustainability   121

Exercise: Video—BP's Level of Corporate Sustainability   124

Strategy Session 19

Monitoring Strategy Implementation Through the Balanced Scorecard   127

Exercise: Everyone Knows the Score When a Major League Baseball Team Ties Performance to Its Mission   129

PART III

Implementing Strategy

Strategy Session 15

Succeeding in Strategy Formulation and Implementation

O B J E C T I V E

To achieve its objectives, an organization must both formulate and implement its strategies. If either of these tasks is done poorly, the result is the likely failure of the overall strategy. This session provides an understanding of both formulation and implementation.

Early writers in the field of strategic management developed rational planning models that distinguished between strategy formulation and strategy implementation. According to the traditional or rational planning framework, strategy formulation was the role of corporate level managers such as the CEO and other senior executives, and it involved developing a strategy that achieved a fit between the external environment (opportunities and threats) and an organization's internal capabilities and resources (strengths and weaknesses). Once a strategy was formulated or developed, its implementation involved a series of subactivities. These included creating an organizational structure to support the company's chosen strategy and designing performance measurement, compensation, incentives, and controls to achieve the kind of management and employee behavior required for successfully executing the strategy.

A revision of the rational planning framework suggests that strategy can emerge in response to unforeseen circumstances. Unplanned responses occur to take advantage of or react to changes in the environment. As a result, the strategies that are implemented look different from what was intended. These effective, but often-unintended, strategies have been labeled *emergent strategies*.

In practice, organizational strategies are probably a combination of the planned and the emergent and often are partially formulated, implemented, and then reformulated to capitalize on strategic opportunities. While it may seem difficult to separate strategy formulation and implementation, since they are closely linked, the two concepts are fundamentally different. In fact, analyzing issues associated with each can provide a useful technique for diagnosing strategic problems.

Framework for Diagnosing Problems. Stated simply, strategy formulation is what you are going to do; strategy implementation is doing it. When an organization chooses to change to a cost leadership strategy (formulation), the execution of that strategy may involve such changes as developing new pricing policies, establishing cost-control procedures, building new facilities, and modifying employee hiring practices and benefits (implementation). If these changes are not carried out successfully, it is impossible to assess the soundness and quality of a given strategy.

The chart in Figure 15.1 shows a way to distinguish between the two concepts in the assessment of strategic performance. The shaded boxes represent the extremes that managers rarely face. In the upper left box, there is outstanding success when the strategy is appropriate and its implementation is sound. All that can be done has been done, and

> I have thought too much to stoop to action.
>
> —*Phillipe Auguste Villiers de L'Isle-Adam*

FIGURE 15.1   DISTINGUISHING STRATEGY FORMULATION AND IMPLEMENTATION

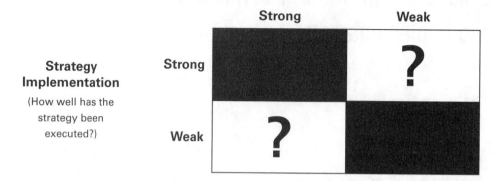

performance indicators are usually strong. The lower right box is exactly the opposite, and performance indicators reveal revenue declines and profit losses. If management tries to improve the strategy, the programs fail because they cannot be executed. If implementation problems are fixed, it results in the execution of a strategy that is not sustainable.

The two question-mark boxes are the ones that practicing managers typically face. The lower left cell involves a situation where the company has chosen a strong strategy that matches organizational resources and capabilities with competitive forces. However, weak implementation will often disguise the appropriateness of the strategy. Because managers are more accustomed to focusing on strategy formulation, the real problem with the strategy (faulty implementation) often is not diagnosed. When performance is low, managers are likely to develop a new strategy rather than question whether the implementation was effective. The new, and perhaps even less appropriate, strategy is then re-implemented and continues to fail.

The upper right box represents situations where an inappropriate strategy is implemented well. The strong execution may overcome the unsound strategy—or at least give management an early warning of impeding problems and the need for a change in strategy. Alternatively, the same strong execution can hasten the failure of the weak strategy. For example, although efficient production and cost-cutting measures may bring an organization to a cost leadership position, this strategy choice may be inappropriate for the target market.

The important point is that diagnosing problems in an organization requires analysis of strategy implementation as well as strategy formulation. It is critical to incorporate both, since strategic soundness cannot be assessed without reviewing issues involving implementation.

Exercise

Diagnosing Problems at Hewlett-Packard

INSTRUCTIONS
Read this short case and then diagnose the problems that occurred at Hewlett-Packard in the questions that follow.

Hewlett-Packard

When Carly Fiorina became CEO of Hewlett-Packard (HP) in 1999, little remained of the founders' entrepreneurial spirit. The company was run by engineers, and CEO Fiorina came to the job with vision and a strategy focus. The board of directors wanted her to declare war on an outdated culture. While the "HP way" pushed authority down into the organization, the board wanted more top-down decisiveness to shake up the old guard. One of Fiorina's major initiatives was a corporate strategy of growth through a $19 billion takeover of Compaq, a company that was the size of HP. Although the merger was bitterly opposed by the heirs of founders Dave Packard and Bill Hewlett, Fiorina had the power of persuasion and stamina to get the board to finally approve the acquisition. The basis for the takeover was that HP could profit by reselling industry-standard computer technologies rather than make is own chips and operating software. HP would add special software to make its Windows/Intel and Linux/Intel computers more desirable than what competitors such as Dell offered.

The takeover plan also included a position for Michael Capellas, the former CEO of Compaq. He was to have primary responsibility for operational or "inside" activities, while Fiorina would handle relations with customers and Wall Street. However, Capellas left the company just a few months after the merger, and Fiorina did not delegate the responsibility for internal operations or find another Capellas. One executive noted that Fiorina tended to pay more attention to inspirational words than to the numbers.

Fiorina also centralized HP's array of businesses. Under her direction, HP was centralized into three product divisions (printers, PCs, and servers). Although these divisions were responsible for designing and building the products, the marketing and sales functions were run by a new and separate division: the Customer Solutions Group. Fiorina formed this group to unite the formerly autonomous product-line groups that made up 80 brands. However, rather than unite all of these groups into one brand, which was the goal, the new structure blocked direct feedback from the sales force to the product designers. Units were at odds trying to get the Customer Solutions Group to devote more sales staff to selling one particular unit's products over another's. Another structural change included combining the technical operation with a global operations group that oversaw $50 billion in spending on everything from ballpoint pens and office furniture to offshore vendor contracts and LCD panels for new notebook computers.

Another example of the centralization plan was that high-ranking HP executives were given control of only 30% of their budgets. In terms of incentives, Fiorina created a complex bonus system built around revenue and profitability. Also included were subjective evaluations such as "total customer experience." What emerged was a high-profile CEO with a top-down management style, as the board originally wanted, but who gave executives less responsibility for internal operations.

Concerns about HP performance began to spread throughout the investment community. By late 2003, investors no longer were preoccupied with the Compaq takeover but instead began to focus on HP's declining competitive position in relation to IBM and Dell. Analysts gave credit to Fiorina's good marketing skills and her strong presence as a spokesperson for HP, but they voiced concerns about operations and the company's sliding stock price. Analysts noted it was time to spin off the PC or printer divisions; however, the board argued that the various businesses were better off under one roof.

Analysts also expressed concerns about the company's lack of innovation, which had been a hallmark of HP. The last noteworthy invention was the company's inkjet printers 20 years ago. Investment in R&D totaled more than 10% of HP sales in the early 1990s but had fallen to 4% in 2005.

By 2004, the board of directors began holding conferences without Fiorina to discuss her performance. At the next board meeting—which was supposed to be an annual strategy review—the focus became the performance of Fiorina and the company. During the meeting, a plan to distribute some of Fiorina's operating responsibilities to key executives was developed, and the result was that Fiorina was fired on February 9, 2005. In her five and a half years as CEO, HP's stock fell 56%.

Mark Hurd, the former CEO of NCR Corp., was named CEO in 2005. By 2007 he had established a position as the "unCarly." He arrived on the job with no grand proclamations but instead spent hours reviewing the books, interrogating the senior staff, and analyzing every detail to get a clear answer about shaving costs and increasing demand. While Fiorina would schmooze with world leaders and high-level business executives, Hurd was more likely to spend a day working the floor at Best Buy near the company's headquarters in Palo Alto, California, to hear how customers viewed HP products. To undo the organizational chaos and bloated costs left by Fiorina, Hurd required dozens of managers to outline in no more than two slides what their group did inside HP and where could they find growth. He memorized all of the metrics—prices, costs, margins, discounts, growth rates, revenues, profits—and reiterated them in follow-up sessions. News of these meetings spread throughout the management, and the message was clear: Understand how revenue moves through your business and how your business fits into HP. Hurd returned budget control to the product division heads. He also imposed layoffs of over 15,000 people. Through 2007, printers continued to lead HP's profitability, other products became more profitable, and the stock price continued to rise.

1. Describe the strategy developed for Hewlett-Packard by Carly Fiorina. Was it a strong or weak strategy? (To determine if the strategy was strong or weak, review whether it dealt with environmental trends and whether it would offset company weaknesses or capitalize upon company strengths.)

_____

_____

_____

_____

_____

2. Identify ways the strategy was implemented. Was it executed well? Discuss.

_____

_____

_____

_____

3. What additional information would you like to be able to judge formulation and implementation better?

_____

_____

_____

_____

4. In the chart below, place an "X" in the cell that best depicts the Hewlett-Packard situation when Fiorina was CEO.

Strategy Formulation

	Strong	Weak
Strong		
Weak		

Strategy Implementation

Strategy Session 16
Structuring to Support Strategy

> **OBJECTIVE**
> Changes in corporate strategy often require changes in the way an organization is structured. In this strategy session, practice designing new structures and systems for a business as its strategy evolves.

An organization's structure is the formal definition of working relationships between people and departments in an organization. Companies often create organizational charts to show who reports to whom and how tasks are divided up. Different structures are required to implement different strategies, and typically structures are changed when they no longer provide the coordination and control necessary to implement strategies successfully.

Form follows function.

—Louis H. Sullivan, founder of the Chicago School of Architecture, in 1896

Management historian Alfred Chandler conducted one of the classic studies dealing with the strategy and organizational structure relationship. After studying U.S. corporations, such as Sears, General Motors, DuPont, and others, Chandler found evidence that when companies changed their strategies, they changed their structures. That is, management set up departments and divisions within the organization to pursue specific strategies, and Chandler labeled this process "structure follows strategy."

Organizational Structures. Although there are many structural forms, there are common types in modern organizations. The first is a simple structure where the owner-manager makes all major decisions directly and coordinates all activities. This structure is appropriate for a small, entrepreneurial firm with one or two product lines following a focused cost leadership or a focused differentiation strategy. Employees tend to be generalists.

As companies grow and add several product lines in one industry, the range of tasks that must be performed expands and no one person can successfully perform more than one organizational task without becoming overloaded. The owner-manager, for example, can no longer make and sell the expanded product lines. Employees tend to be specialists in the business functions and are grouped into departments, such as marketing, production, accounting and finance, and human resources, as shown in the simplified organizational chart shown in Figure 16.1. The task of the CEO is to ensure that communication and coordination exists among the departments and that the actions of the departments benefit the entire organization.

Once a corporation diversifies into more than one industry, the multidivisional structure is used. It better equips the organization to handle corporate strategies, which deal with the question of what businesses to be in. As a company expands and diversifies, it becomes more difficult for the CEO to process increasing quantities of strategic information. Therefore, responsibilities for day-to-day operations are delegated to division managers. Employees tend to be functional specialists grouped according to product and market distinctions. How autonomous the divisions are varies from company to company.

FIGURE 16.1   FUNCTIONAL STRUCTURE

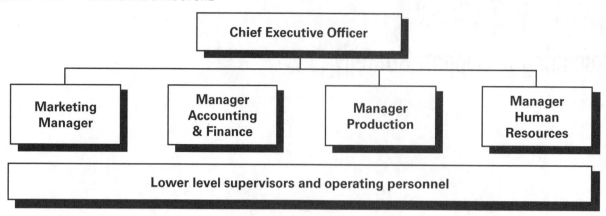

When organizations expand into many areas of business with dozens of different products and markets, the diversity and number of divisions can cause the CEO problems in strategic planning and control as well as overseeing operations. The span of control becomes too large. The solution is to combine several divisions into product groups or strategic business units (SBUs), each under one executive, such as a group vice president. The CEO then can manage the divisions through this level of vice presidents. An example of a strategic business unit organizational chart is shown in Figure 16.2.

FIGURE 16.2   SBU STRUCTURE

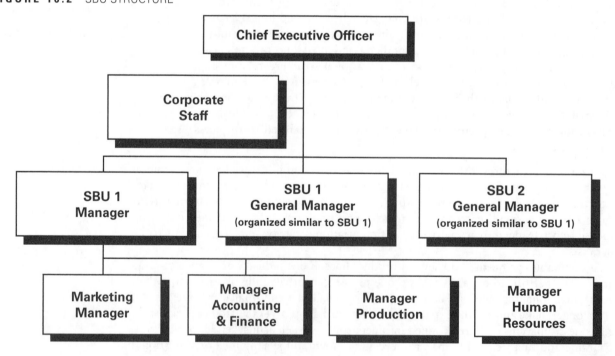

As strategies change, other structures have emerged to serve specific organizational needs. Organizations that manage several projects often use a complex matrix design, which is a hybrid of the functional and the divisional structures as shown in Figure 16.3. Employees literally work in two departments and have two supervisors. For example, an employee in the marketing department reports to the head of marketing but also reports to a product or project manager. Another unique structure is a network-type form, often termed a "nonstructure." In a network, or "virtual organization" as it is also called, companies outsource many activities traditionally handled by employees of the organization and thus eliminate in-house business departments.

FIGURE 16.3 MATRIX DESIGN STRUCTURE

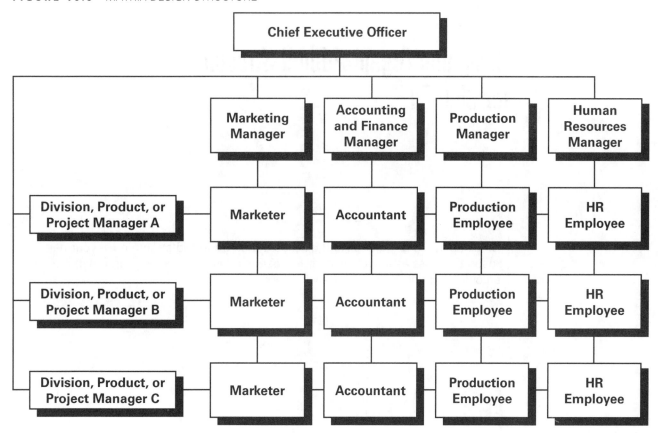

Exercise

Designing Organizational Structures for Club Ed

INSTRUCTIONS

Break up into small groups and discuss the strategy and structure for your new resort business as it evolves over the periods described below—and then create an overhead transparency for each period.

Team Activity

Period I

Determined never to shovel snow again, you are establishing a new resort business on a small Caribbean island. Construction is under way, and the resort is scheduled to open a year from now. You decide it is time to draw up an organizational chart for this new venture, Club Ed. Your initial workforce consists of 15 employees.

1. Develop your generic strategy. Who is the target market? What will be your competitive advantage (cost leadership or differentiation)?

2. What jobs do you need to have covered? What tasks need to be done? What services will you provide?

Work in your group to draw your organizational chart and be prepared to discuss your generic strategy and the components and rationale for your company structure.

Your instructor will select one or two groups to present their designs and lead the class discussion.

Adapted from Cheryl Harvey and Kim Morouney. 1998. Organizational Structure and Design: The Club Ed Exercise. *Journal of Management Education* 22(3): 425-430. Used with permission.

Team Activity
Period II

You are into your tenth year of operation; Club Ed is wildly successful and you would not recognize a snow shovel if you saw one! You and your partners own 30 Club Eds in a variety of locations in South America, Central America, North America, the Caribbean, and the South Pacific, and the total number of employees is over 400. What are the biggest problems to date? Have you dealt with them in your structure? How have your human resource, control, and information systems developed? Draw an up-to-date organizational chart and prepare to explain your rationale to your classmates.

Your instructor will select one or two groups to present their designs and lead the class discussion.

Team Activity
Period III

Ten more years pass. The Club is now in 50 locations and operates three cruise ships. The fleet of "Love Boats" offers seven-day cruises to the Caribbean, Alaska, and the Far East. Ships include casinos, live music, dancing, nightclubs, and a selection of movies. Food is available around the clock in the main dining rooms. A recent customer profile shows that almost 50% of customers are repeat business and are 40 years and older. The three "Ss" (sun, sand or snow, and sex) marketing theme no longer appeals to this population in a world where AIDS and fears of skin cancer are all too real. Reservations have been down over the past several seasons as economic conditions fluctuate. How does Club Ed restructure to adapt?

Your instructor will select one or two groups to present their designs and lead the class discussion.

Discussion Questions

1. What is the relationship between strategy and structure?
2. How can Club Ed structure itself as an adaptive organization? Does it always have to react to environmental changes or are there some ways it can be proactive?

Notes

_____

_____

_____

_____

_____

_____

_____

Strategy Session 17

Strategy Implementation Using the 7-S Model

OBJECTIVE

This session will help you recognize the actions that are needed in different areas of the organization to implement strategy. The 7-S Model provides the framework for examining the actions and appreciating the interrelationships between them.

Effective strategic management requires that an organization have a good strategy, and that its members make it work as well. Implementing strategy involves coordinating a broad range of changes that interrelate. Making limited changes seldom brings any significant overall organizational effect. To redirect organizations, managers must deal with several overlapping and related issues.

If the various parts and processes of an organization are all in complete alignment, it is reflected in the organization's performance. A useful way of visualizing these various components and their alignment is through the "7-S Model." The model was developed by McKinsey & Company, a consulting firm, as a framework for thinking about effective management and for bringing about change in an organization. By presenting an integrated view of an organization, the 7-S Model is a useful mechanism to see the interplay between the various elements in the process of implementation. The 7-S framework consists of the following:

> The value of a strategy depends not only on the elegance of its conception but fully as much on whether the company proposing the strategy can really execute it.
>
> —*Robert H. Waterman, Jr.*

1. **Strategy.** That set of decisions and actions by which the organization plans to gain competitive advantage, and which determines its long-term performance.
2. **Structure.** The organization chart and other means by which an organization divides the tasks to be performed and simultaneously ensures its coordination.
3. **Systems.** Procedures (both formal and informal) through which the organization functions on a daily basis. These include budgeting systems, information systems, quality control systems, production scheduling, etc.
4. **Style.** The culture, or values and beliefs of the organization, as revealed in the way its members behave.
5. **Staff.** The human resources of the organization, including recruitment, training, compensation, morale, and so on.
6. **Superordinate goals (or shared values).** Abstract guiding concepts of an organization, shared by most employees. These are sometimes captured in its mission statement, but may go beyond formally stated objectives.
7. **Skills.** The capabilities of the organization that collectively can be claimed as its competencies.

The basic message of the model is that (1) many factors exist that determine an organization's success; (2) all of them must complement each other; and (3) they are all equally important. Since all factors are equally important, there is no start or finish to the model.

To use the model to examine implementation, one needs to identify the strategy and then assess whether the other elements are consistent with it, and if not, what changes need to be made. For instance, if an organization's strategy calls for innovation and better product development, then actions in the "Staff" area should ensure that people with the right skills are hired and rewarded. The "Systems" should ensure that the monitoring measures track product development. The "Structure" must allow the product development department to access the information it needs and have the authority to make the decisions it needs to make. The "Style" should encourage more risk taking.

Poor implementation can make the best designed strategies fail. Hence, the formulation and implementation of strategy can rarely be separated and together is referred to as the formation of strategy. Poor implementation has also been identified as a major cause for failure of mergers and acquisitions. While the strategy may call for two organizations to be joined, lack of consideration of how the two cultures will fit, whether the systems can be integrated, and so on could easily result in the M&A unraveling.

Exercise

Transition at PeopleSoft

PeopleSoft, Inc.

PeopleSoft, Inc., a California-based software company, was one of three major players in the over $20 billion enterprise resource planning software (ERP) industry. The other two were SAP AG of Germany, and Oracle Corp. The ERP industry provided the integrated software that drove big corporations. These applications included financial software for accounting, human resource programs for personnel administration, and manufacturing packages to automate production—the goal being to improve efficiencies for the client's entire enterprise.

On an average, a PeopleSoft product cost $1 million. The company initially grew rapidly, at a rate of 111% between 1990 and 1995. Revenues in 1998 were $1.3 billion, 12 times that of 1994. PeopleSoft was the only one of the three players that relied entirely on enterprise software for its success. Its main customers were midmarket companies that made less than $750 million in annual revenues—a niche PeopleSoft dominated.

PeopleSoft's Origins

David A Duffield, a former sales executive at IBM, saw an opportunity to develop client-server systems that linked individual PCs to a bigger computer serving the whole office. He founded PeopleSoft in 1987 along with a software designer, Ken Morris, and profited from the shift from mainframe computing to networking. PeopleSoft pioneered business management applications that were able to run on all kinds of systems, and was the first company to do so using Microsoft Windows. The number of employees grew from 914 in 1994 to 7,032 in 1999.

Like most software companies, PeopleSoft built an informal and sensitive corporate culture. David Duffield became a cult figure within his company. His initials, DAD, suited him appropriately for his role. He routinely schmoozed with workers, and a company rock band was named after him—the Raving Daves. Employees saw him as easygoing and not a typical CEO. The company developed its own company lingo where people ate company funded "PeopleSnacks," and shopped at the company "PeopleStore."

The office sometimes had a fun, "theme park" atmosphere. Games took place spontaneously. There was no dress code. Managers did not have secretaries. Giant posters of smiling employees lined the hallways shouting out messages such as "Just try to get me to leave!" Duffield stressed that the company was more than just making money. It was about having fun and having a heart. Duffield considered himself a family man; he had seven children, of whom four were adopted.

The company's personnel policies were considered family friendly too. Fifty-eight percent of new PeopleSoft hires came through an employee referral service program that actively encouraged workers to recruit relatives and friends. Duffield's wife, Cheryl, helped found PeopleSoft, and his brother, son, and daughter all worked there. Dozens of married couples and relatives worked within the company ranks. The company had a "Bring your parents to work" day.

PeopleSoft shunned bureaucracy. Executives answered their own phones and wrote their own letters. Employees were encouraged to say what they thought and made important decisions without frequently going to others for help. "Don't ask for permission, ask for forgiveness if something goes wrong" was a company belief. The staff often worked 70-hour weeks. PeopleSoft also had attractive benefits and an employee stock purchase plan. Employees received a company laptop to use and were free to telecommute from home.

Duffield said the company's main goal was to keep its customers happy and spared no expense for that. More than one-third of the company's 1,000 employees were directly involved in customer service. Sometimes, the effort went beyond the call of duty, such as when a PeopleSoft representative helped a Florida-based company get back in business following a devastating hurricane. The PeopleSoft technician even flew back to Miami on Christmas Day since the company had to have its system up and running by the end of the year.

Duffield maintained that the key challenge, through its rapid growth, was retaining their corporate culture. "Other companies would kill for the kind of commitment we have—and it is primarily due to the culture of the company." However, as the company grew rapidly and the number of employees rose, many newcomers did not feel as much a part of the family as the older employees did. The rapid growth hurt products too. The designers from human resources and manufacturing became focused on their own areas, and the products each group produced did not look alike and work together as well as they should have for an integrated management software offering. Bugs in programs began to increase, and customers started complaining of poor service. "When you're growing at 80 to 90% a year, you can make mistakes," Duffield said. "They get covered up."

Continued Growth

The acquisitions of other software companies supported PeopleSoft's growth. In 1996, PeopleSoft acquired Red Pepper Software, but Duffield kept the two organizations separate to protect Red Pepper's brand identity and to alleviate any negative impact the new acquisition would have on PeopleSoft's corporate culture. However, the communication between the two companies was very poor. Analysts felt that PeopleSoft needed to quickly integrate and to avoid a negative influence on its bottom line.

Then the ERP industry began to suddenly experience the bad times that virtually every sector of the IT industry faced beginning in the late 1990s and subsequent recession of 2001. While analysts forecasted a market of $52 billion in ERP sales by 2002, as the year 2000 approached, firms began focusing on Y2K issues (i.e., computer software issues in the transition to the year 2000) and sales began to taper off. SAP, the lead player with about one-third market share, saw its stock price fall from $80 in mid-1998 to $23 in a year. Focused on rapid growth, PeopleSoft did not see the slowing trend. Revenue from new product sales fell 60% and the stock price that had been approaching $60 a share in April 1998 dropped to $11 a year later.

In 1999, PeopleSoft reacted with layoffs that most people thought would never happen in the "family." Some managers wept in departmental meetings while planning how to conduct the layoffs. Some were informed over voicemail, others were not given any explanation, and one employee was called in the middle of her vacation and told not to return. Yet, in a company chat room, postings did not generate expressions of anger or frustration from current or departing employees, just support for the company and Duffield. The employee turnover rate that used to be barely 5% a year rose to 20%.

A new CEO, Craig Conway, was appointed by the end of the year. His prior experience was in the software industry, including eight years at Oracle Corporation in a variety of roles including marketing, sales, and operations. Conway, who wore a tie, promised that the casual dress code and egalitarianism would remain. He said he would bring "mature management," "predictability," and "accountability" to the company, and would focus on providing more innovative technology, greater flexibility, faster implementation, lower costs, and better customer support than PeopleSoft's rivals. While pursuing the same overall strategy, Conway had growth plans in the areas of e-commerce and software systems for smaller companies. With ERP slowing, other markets were looking attractive. The American business-to-consumer and business-to-business e-commerce markets were to grow significantly. The company was also in the process of acquiring JD Edwards & Co., which developed and marketed collaborative enterprise software and consulting, education, and support services. JD Edwards was about half the size of PeopleSoft. Conway's goal was to increase PeopleSoft revenues to $5 billion by 2005.

Commenting on Conway's appointment as CEO, Duffield noted that the culture lacked accountability. He felt that the company needed people who committed to something and then got it done and said Conway could achieve that. Duffield remained as chairman of the board, taking part in strategic decisions and spending time building relationships with customers and employees.

Name: _____

Directions: Reflect on the case, and respond, under "Actions I" below, what you would initiate if you were Conway. Then await further instructions.

Strategy (Actions planned in response to or in anticipation of changes in the external environment—customers and competition.)

Actions I:

Actions II:

Superordinate Goals (Guiding concepts, a set of values and aspirations, often unwritten, that may go beyond formally stated objectives. They are succinct, abstract, and mean a lot to insiders.)

Actions I:

Actions II:

Structure (The division of tasks and its coordination within the company.)

Actions I:

Actions II:

Systems (All the procedures, formal and informal, that make the organization work: budgeting systems, training systems, accounting systems, etc.)

Actions I:

Actions II:

Style (A representation of the organization's culture, it reflects the values and beliefs as demonstrated in symbolic behavior.)

Actions I:

Actions II:

Staff (The people issues, both hard—pay scales, training programs, etc.—and soft—morale, attitude, motivation, etc.)

Actions I:

Actions II:

Skills (Crucial attributes of the company, its strengths, and competencies.)

Actions I:

Actions II:

Strategy Session 18
Corporate Sustainability

> **OBJECTIVE**
> Understand corporate sustainability and its connection to corporate social responsibility.

From the 1970s and through the 1980s, questions arose about the obligation of organizations toward society. Company mission statements began to incorporate commitments to some level of social responsibility, and annual reports often included discussions of what was done during the year to demonstrate the company's attention to the ideal of social performance in addition to economic performance.

During that timeframe, the idea of corporate social responsibility became part of management study. Two viewpoints guided the level and type of involvement management undertook in terms of activities to benefit society.

> How to balance the common good and the special purpose of the institution is the question we must answer.
>
> —*Peter F. Drucker*

The Classical Economic Approach. This approach argued for a low level of involvement in social activities, unless there was a direct benefit to the bottom line. It called for the role of management to focus on activities that improved the economic performance of the firm and that resulted in profits for the owners (stockholders). According to the economist Milton Friedman, a strong proponent of this view, a potential conflict of interest existed when society held managers responsible to owners for meeting profit goals, yet at the same time held them responsible to society to enhance the social welfare. Every dollar spent on social problems or donated to a charity was one fewer dollar distributed to the owners in the form of dividends and one fewer dollar for the kind of investment needed to build a firm's competitive position. In summary, management's sole responsibility should be to follow legal and ethical rules of society while maximizing profitability.

The Activist Approach. This approach argued for a high level of involvement in social activities because business is a part of society and therefore has an obligation to deal with social issues. This framework sees business as a corporate citizen with the technical, financial, and managerial resources to help solve society's difficult problems. Managers have an obligation to respond to the needs of all stakeholders while pursuing a profit. This framework calls for business to advance both societal and economic objectives.

Until the 1990s, corporate social responsibility remained a mixture of both approaches. Some firms, such as Ben & Jerry's, had strong preferences toward the activist approach. However, in most organizations the costs of pursuing a socially responsible activity versus the consequences of not doing so were taken into account, along with the personality and preferences of the top management team. As a result, the involvement in social responsibility activities varied widely among corporations.

Corporate Sustainability and the Environment

A major shift in corporate responsibility to sustainability began in the 1990s, with increased emphasis throughout the 2000s. The concept began to take hold as a result of the 1987 publication of the World Commission on Environment and Development report entitled *Our Common Future*. In this report, sustainability was defined as development that meets the needs of the present without compromising the ability of future generations to meet their own needs. The report noted that corporations have been the engines for economic development, and it was critical for management to be more proactive in balancing the drive for profit with social equity and environmental protection, partly because corporations have caused some of the unsustainable conditions and also because they have the access to resources needed to address the problems. In the report, both public and private organizations were charged with becoming better stewards of the environment and with promoting positive economic growth and social objectives. The old concept of corporate social responsibility, which blended both economic and social components, was replaced by corporate sustainability that included a third element—the environment.

By the time Al Gore's movie, *An Inconvenient Truth*, (a documentary that described the damage to the environment and what needs to be done) was released in 2006, the concepts of "going green" and "green initiatives" were part of management's vocabulary and were familiar to virtually every employee and consumer.

Strategic Management and Sustainability

From a strategy perspective, corporate sustainability is in line with strategic management and the stakeholder approach in particular. First developed by R. Edward Freeman, the basic premise of stakeholder theory is that strong relationships with external groups make it easier to meet corporate objectives and to achieve a competitive advantage when those relationships are built on trust, respect, and cooperation. Many stakeholder groups can be identified, although the most frequently discussed are stockholders and investors, employees, customers, and suppliers. The goals of economic stability, environmental protection, and social justice are common across these groups, and stakeholder theory suggests it is in the company's best economic interest to develop strategies that meet stakeholder goals.

Today, most business writers and scholars agree that sustainability is more than "another thing to do." The principles of sustainability can stimulate technological innovation, advance competitiveness, and improve the quality of life. The extent to which a company incorporates sustainability has strategic management implications.

Ad-hoc Level. For many firms, a more informal or ad-hoc approach to incorporating sustainability is taken as a starting point. For example, this level might include one or two stand-alone sustainability initiatives that are not connected to strategic objectives of the company. The reason for these initiatives can be to improve the company's profit through increased efficiencies or as a means of demonstrating leadership and improving the company's image and reputation. Without a more formalized approach to ensure long-standing commitment, however, these initiatives can fade as attention is focused on other issues.

Part of the Strategic Management Process. A formalized approach includes statements by the company as to its understanding of corporate sustainability and the level to which it commits. Frequently sustainability objectives are outlined in formal reports, as in the case of Hewlett-Packard. In its Global Citizenship Report—and prominently displayed on its Web site—HP outlines three priorities: 1) sustainability improvement through the supply chain; 2) minimizing the impact of climate change associated with HP operations and the supply chain while innovating products and solutions for an energy- and carbon-constrained world; and 3) increasing the volume of HP products recovered for reuse and recycling. The Global Citizenship Report identifies specific goals and shows performance toward these goals. This latter piece (showing performance toward goals) is a key component of strategy implementation. Performance metrics demonstrate what a company has done versus its intentions.

Other examples include PepsiCo's Sustainability Report, which includes goals and progress reporting in the areas of corporate sustainability, human sustainability, environmental sustainability, and talent sustainability; and John Deere's Global Sustainability Report, which includes sustainability as part of the firm's mission, values, product development, employee involvement, dealer participation, and charitable contributions.

UN Global Compact. Companies such as HP and John Deere produce the reports noted above because they are members of the UN Global Compact. The United Nations has taken the lead in this area by identifying 10 universally accepted principles dealing with areas such as labor, human rights, environment, and anti-corruption. Once a company decides to adopt the compact, it requires endorsement by its board of directors, and the principles are expected to become a part of the strategy and operations of the company. The company is also required to publish an annual report on progress made. Information about the UN Global Compact can be found at http://www.unglobalcompany.org/.

Exercise: Video

BP's Level of Corporate Sustainability

1. Write a mission statement for BP that reflects the company's core purpose and its understanding of its corporate sustainability.

_____

_____

_____

_____

_____

2. At what level of corporate sustainability is BP? Briefly describe.

_____

_____

_____

_____

_____

3. Describe whether BP is meeting the economic, social, and environmental goals typically associated with corporate sustainability.

_____

_____

_____

_____

4. What information would you like to see in this video that convinces you to believe in BPs commitment to sustainability?

_____

_____

_____

Strategy Session 19

Monitoring Strategy Implementation Through the Balanced Scorecard

> **OBJECTIVE**
> This session illustrates how a balanced scorecard links the organization's mission and strategy to performance measures.

It is not unusual for planning teams to spend months crafting a mission statement, analyzing environments, and developing strategic initiatives only to find that few strategic changes occur as expected. Although external factors, such as economic downturns or competitive actions may affect the execution of intended strategies, the majority of strategic plans break down because of ineffective implementation. Typically, this is due to no measurable definitions for success from an operational standpoint.

> If you can measure that of which you speak and express it in numbers, you know something about your subject; but if you cannot measure it, your knowledge is of a very meager and unsatisfactory kind.
>
> —*Lord Kelvin*

The balanced scorecard, developed by Kaplan and Norton, is a performance measurement and strategic management system that looks at more than just financial measures to evaluate an organization's progress toward achieving its mission. As one executive noted, "When I receive financial reports, I am either happy or upset, but rarely am I smarter." By incorporating other operational perspectives in the scoring system, the balanced scorecard reflects continuous improvement in management thought and learning about how to better strategically manage organizations.

The balanced scorecard suggests that implementation of the organization's mission and strategies be viewed from four perspectives and that metrics be developed in each of the following areas.

Customers. Customer measures focus on how an organization is viewed by its customers. While most companies recognize the importance of customer perception, the balanced scorecard forces managers to turn general goals, such as increasing customer satisfaction, into specific, measurable characteristics. A manufacturing organization's scorecard might include customer measures such as delivery time, defect rates, number of returns, warranty claims, or customer satisfaction ratings. These measures help managers to evaluate their performance through the customers' eyes, while also benchmarking their performance against industry leaders and standards.

Business Processes. Business processes deal with existing operations to determine where the organization must excel to become successful. It helps find the processes that are critical for satisfying customer needs. Typically, business processes include:

- Building the company by spurring innovation to develop new products and services and to penetrate new markets and customer segments.
- Achieving operational excellence by improving supply chain management and other internal processes to improve costs and quality of the operation.
- Increasing customer value by expanding relationships with existing customers.

Human Resources. These measures evaluate the return on intellectual assets, education and training, innovation, morale, and other human-resource-related factors to evaluate how well the organization is implementing its strategies. Typical metrics might include measures of employee satisfaction, employee turnover, absenteeism, and the percentage of employee suggestions implemented.

Financial Perspective. The financial perspective traditionally has been the focus of performance measurement systems. For organizations adopting the balanced scorecard approach, financial performance measures are used in tandem with the customer, business processes, and human resource measures. Typical indicators include cash flow, return on equity, sales, and income growth.

The balanced scorecard in diagram form in Figure 19.1 shows the mission at the heart of the scoring system. Surrounding the mission are specific measurements grouped according to the perspectives described above. All of the boxes are connected by arrows to illustrate the integration of these areas. Achieving one perspective's targets should lead to desired improvements in the next perspective, and so on. The example of a financial institution such as a credit union, which serves the financial needs of its members, illustrates the scorecard approach.

FIGURE 19.1 BALANCED SCORECARD

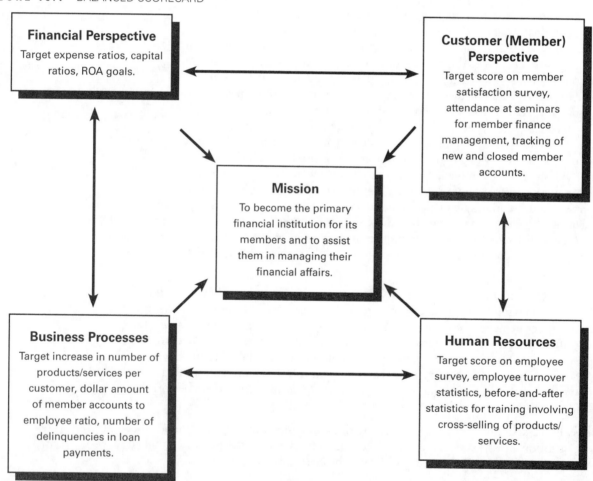

Exercise

Everyone Knows the Score When a Major League Baseball Team Ties Performance to Its Mission

INSTRUCTIONS

Review the mission statement developed by the Colorado Rockies Major League Baseball team and identify specific performance measures as they relate to the mission.

Colorado Rockies Mission Statement

The Colorado Rockies is a sports business with a team value of $371 million as of 2007. The team generated revenues of $145 million and income of $16.3 million in 2005. Its mission statement is:

To provide the highest level of baseball entertainment in an excellent stadium environment at prices affordable for families, and to support the development of youth baseball throughout the Rocky Mountain region.

The statement clearly identifies the fans' needs. First and foremost, it is baseball entertainment. By being very clear about the team's mission, the statement provides a foundation for strategies and new activities. If management is looking for ways to increase attendance, its focus is on enhancing the baseball entertainment experience of fans. For example, new activities could be added to the program, such as fireworks after home runs or the creation of "grandstand manager nights" when fans in the stands—not the Rockies' manager—decide whether the players on the field would bunt (purposely tap the ball only a few yards using the barrel of the bat), steal a base by running to the next base when the pitcher is delivering a pitch, or what pitches would be thrown (fastball, slider, change-up, and the like.). However, activities are not performance measures, and specific targets are needed to ensure that the energies, abilities, and specific knowledge of people throughout the sports organization are linked to its mission.

Complete the table in Figure 19.2. Identify at least three specific measures in each of the areas shown. The mission components have been separated and labeled a, b, c, or d:

a. Highest level of baseball entertainment

b. Excellent stadium environment

c. Prices affordable to families

d. Support of youth baseball

For each measure, identify which element(s) of the mission relate to the measure. An example is given in each section.

FIGURE 19.2 MISSION MEASURES AND ELEMENTS

Measures	Mission Elements
Financial perspective	1. Revenue target (a, c) 2. 3. 4.
Customers	1. Number of fans' visits per season (a) 2. 3. 4.
Business processes	1. Stadium sound levels (b) 2. 3. 4.
Human resources	1. Employee turnover rates (a, b) 2. 3. 4.

1. Briefly explain how measurement in the customers area may affect business processes or human resources.

_____

_____

_____

_____

_____

_____

2. How easy or difficult is it to identify measures for the four quadrants?

_____

_____

_____

_____

_____

_____

_____

3. How important is technology and information systems for the success of the balanced scorecard system?

_____

_____

_____

_____

_____

_____

Lodging Industry Profile   135

Template for Industry Survey   139

Assessing Strategic Performance Through
Financial Analysis   141

Case Study 1
Strategic Alternatives at Mercury
Telecom   143

Case Study 2
Caffeine Satisfaction: Rivalry Among the
Coffee Shops   149

PART IV
Industry Analysis

Lodging
Industry Profile

As a result of a better balance between the supply and demand of hotel rooms, the industry's average daily room rate rose over 5% from 2003 to 2007. On the supply side, the number of rooms added ranged from 1–2%, which is lower than the 3–4% increase that occurred in the late 1990s. On the demand side, in 2006 and 2007, business and vacation travelers increased hotel occupancy, both from the U.S. and overseas. However, during the latter half of 2008, the economy declined and demand decreased; and similar forecasts are projected through 2010.

Industry Overview

The lodging industry provides accommodations for travelers while they are away from home. Individuals traveling for business totaled 44% in 2006, and 56% were leisure travelers. The business travelers are primarily male, age 35–54, have managerial or professional positions, and have household incomes of $85,900 on average. Leisure travelers are in the same age range and travel primarily by automobile.

The business travelers' needs include basic room essentials, meal services, and communication facilities such as fax machines and in-room Internet access. In addition, meeting rooms, duplicating services, and recreational and entertainment options are frequently desired. Business guests most often travel alone, make reservations, and pay on average $112 per room night.

Nonbusiness travelers look for the basic accommodations of bed, bath, telephone, and sometimes meal services. If the location is a destination resort, travelers expect extensive leisure and recreational facilities. Increases in fuel prices, however, can negatively impact consumer travel behavior. Drivers must pay higher gas prices and airlines must add fuel surcharges, and car rental agencies must increase rates to cover the added fuel costs. Price fluctuations and the state of the economy quickly affect the amount of personal travel, whereas business travel follows turns in the economy by three to six months. The typical nonbusiness consumer travels in pairs and pays on average $103 per room night.

At the close of 2007, the U.S. lodging industry consisted of 50,000 properties with a total of 4.54 million rooms. Revenues totaled $142.6 billion, which is a 6.9% increase from 2006. While lower demand and greater supply is expected adversely to affect average daily room rates and revenue per available room, Table A.1 shows that the lodging industry is in a relatively healthy position.

Industry Competitors

Although the lodging industry consists of establishments that range from luxurious five-star hotels to youth hostels and RV parks, hotels and motels are the major components. In general, these properties are classified as full-service or limited service. Full-service establishments offer a variety of services, and most include at least one or more restaurant and beverage service options. These options may range from coffee bars to full restaurants. They also provide room service. A number of full-service hotels have features such as

TABLE A.1 AVERAGE ROOM RATES AND REVENUE PER AVAILABLE ROOM

Year	Average Room Rate	% Change	Occupancy Rate before Revenue per Available Room	Revenue per Available Room*	% Change
2007	103.64	5.9	63.2	65.50	5.7
2006	97.89	7.2	63.3	61.96	7.7
2005	90.91	5.4	63.1	57.37	8.5
2004	86.23	4.0	61.3	52.88	7.8
2003	83.12	0.1	59.2	49.18	0.6
2002	83.01	(1.4)	58.9	48.91	(2.6)

*Average Room Rate × Occupancy Rate

laundry and valet services, fitness centers, and swimming pools. Some luxury hotel chains also manage condominium units in combination with the nightly rate rooms, giving both hotel guests and condominium owners access to the services and amenities.

Limited-service hotels do not have on-site restaurants or most other amenities offered by the full-service establishments. They usually offer continental breakfasts, vending machines, Internet access, and unattended pools or game rooms. The number of these types of properties has been growing, since they are not as costly to build or maintain. In addition, they appeal to budget-conscious families on vacation or travelers who are willing to trade lower room prices for fewer amenities.

In recent years the hotel industry has been dominated by a few large national hotel chains. These properties provide brand recognition, and familiar chain establishments are associated with levels of consistency in terms of quality and pricing. Most of the largest companies and many smaller businesses are publicly owned. The largest U.S. hotel company is Wyndham Worldwide Corporation, which is the parent of nine lodging chains with over 6,500 properties and more than 550,000 rooms. It was created as part of a four-way split of the conglomerate Cendant Corp. in 2006. Under the Wyndham name are Days Inn, Howard Johnson, Knights Inn, Ramada, Travelodge, and Super 8. Table A.2 provides an overview of some of the large hotel establishments.

TABLE A.2 OVERVIEW OF LARGE HOTEL COMPANIES

Company	Major Chains Owned	Properties	Rooms
InterContinental Hotels Group	Holiday Inn, InterContinental	3,949	585,094
Wyndham Worldwide	Days Inn, Ramada, Super 8, Howard Johnson, Travelodge (North America)	6,544	550,576
Marriott International	Marriott, Courtyard Residence Inn, Fairfield Inn, Renaissance	2,999	535,093
Hilton Hotels	Hilton (U.S.), Hampton Inns, Doubletree, Embassy Suites, Homewood Suites	2,940	490,000
Accor S.A.	Motel 6, Mercure, Ibis, Novotel, Red Roof Inns, Hotel Sofitel, Formule 1	3,871	461,698
Choice Hotels International	Comfort Inn, Quality Inn, Econo Lodge	5,570	452,027
Best Western International	Best Western	4,200	316,095
Starwood Hotels & Resorts	Sheraton, Westin	897	274,535

Some major firms remain privately held, such as the Radisson Hotels chain owned by Carlson Companies, and Hyatt Corp., controlled by the Pritzker family. Recently, a number of hotels and casinos have been acquired by private equity firms. For example, in 2007 The Blackstone Group acquired Hilton Hotels.

Although the lodging industry has become more consolidated over time as a result of acquisitions and internal expansion, no single company accounts for more than 15% of all rooms in the United States.

Industry Segments

Market segmentation is dividing a larger market into segments based upon different consumer needs or product preferences, and hotel companies have used segmentation as a way to increase revenues. In the lodging industry, segmentation involves developing different properties to appeal to different types of guests. There are five broad segment types: luxury, upscale, mid-price, economy, and budget. Table A.3 shows the comparison of occupancy levels by segment and location. The trend data for occupancy reveals that properties located on highways and resorts posted declines in average occupancy levels. The resort properties, however, were able to sustain the decline with a 5.6% increase in room rates versus the highway properties that had only a 2.4% increase in room rates.

TABLE A.3 LODGING SEGMENT DATA

Segment	Occupancy 2007	Occupancy 2002	Room Rate 2007	Room Rate 2002
By price				
Luxury	70.9%	67.2%	$168.88	$138.41
Upscale	64.8%	63.2%	113.56	91.26
Mid-price	60.4%	58.4%	92.18	68.61
Economy	57.7%	55.9%	61.29	54.42
Budget	59.4%	57.0%	50.57	42.72
By location				
Urban	68.6%	63.8%	$148.93	$121.66
Suburban	63.4%	61.1%	90.07	79.99
Airport	69.5%	63.4%	99.67	77.31
Highway	58.0%	58.1%	66.93	65.38
Resort	66.1%	61.9%	143.19	135.57

Despite these strong occupancy rates through 2007, it is expected that industry demand will be nearly flat in 2008, which will result in an overall occupancy rate decline. While the upper end and lower end segments are expected to maintain occupancy levels, the decline in consumer discretionary income as well as high gas prices will affect the mid-price segment, which includes brands such as Hilton, Sheraton, and Marriott.

Service Offerings

Lodging businesses are tailoring their products and services to the customers they wish to attract. For example, hotel companies offer voice mail services and in-room Internet access that appeal to business travelers. Extended-stay hotels, which provide services aimed at guests seeking a room for a least five nights, feature separate living room areas and kitchen facilities. Another hotel company, Marriott International, moved into the management of retirement communities, where the company is applying its experience in facilities management and providing hospitality to consumers.

Marketing and Technology

E-commerce and the use of the Internet to contact properties directly are technological developments that will continue to help smooth sales and the delivery of lodging services. Internet addresses and home pages for hotel chains and for individual properties provide direct access to information about facilities that customers can use to perform their own research in making lodging choices when they or their employees travel. In addition, the use of the Internet for booking reservations will continue to grow.

Technology is also enhancing the marketing efforts of hotel firms. These companies are using data about how many times a guest stayed at the hotel and what services were used to differentiate the level and types of services provided. Hotel companies are also creating marketing affiliations to boost sales. For example, cross-marketing arrangements with airlines provide consumers with frequent flyer miles for staying at certain hotels.

Employment

Work in hotels ranges from demanding and hectic at peak times to slow and tiresome during off-season and overnight periods. The type of jobs include management positions, accountants, chefs, waiters and waitresses, janitors, maids and housekeeping cleaners, landscaping and groundskeeping workers, baggage porters and bellhops, among others. Through 2016, employment in this industry is expected to increase by 14%. The number of hotel, motel, and resort desk clerks is expected to grow faster than any occupation because even the limited-service hotels will require desk clerks. Employment of waiters and waitresses will grow more slowly. This reflects the increasing number of limited-service properties that do not have onsite restaurants or that contract the food component to outside sources.

Approximately 10% of workers in hotels are covered by union contracts compared to 13% of workers in all industries combined.

Industry Outlook

The lodging industry is in the mature stage of its life cycle. This is evidenced by the segmentation strategies being developed by key players and the increasing consolidation of the industry. The construction of new properties and additions to existing hotels will remain low, which will help the industry to withstand decreases in demand due to economic conditions the next few years.

Template
for Industry Survey

An industry survey provides important information to understand why firms follow the strategies they do. It also provides management with needed data in formulating competitive strategies. This template will help you gather the information in a systematic manner to create an industry profile. Once all of the information is gathered, it provides the framework for further analysis of industry trends and competitive strategies.

Industry Overview

1. **Identification/definition of the industry**
   Brief description of the products or services produced by competitors in the industry, major players, SIC code.

2. **Origin of industry**
   Historical description including events that affected its profitability, major inventions/innovations that affected the industry.

3. **Location of industry**
   Initial location of the industry, whether geographical clusters exist, importance of being close to markets or inputs.

4. **Globalization trends**
   World Trade Organization requirements and national considerations, intergovernmental agreements, preferential trading arrangements.

Players in the Industry

1. **Size of firms in the industry**
   Sales, capacity and asset base of firms, existence of a minimum efficient size of plant, trends in concentration.

2. **Organizational structures**
   Nature of organizational forms in the industry, private vs. public ownership.

3. **Industry restructuring**
   Trends in restructuring of firms in the industry, tendency to diversify, backward/forward integrate, and reasons for the same.

4. **Interfirm arrangements**
   Extent of cooperation within the industry, alliances, joint R&D projects, activities of the trade association, lobbying efforts and relations with the government.

5. **Substitute industry(ies)**
   Are there substitute products or services from another industry that appear to be different but can satisfy the same need (for example, bottled water as a substitute for cola, fax as a substitute for shipping via UPS, and wine as a substitute for beer)?

Other Industry Characteristics

1. **Value creation methods and costs**
   Description of production/value creation process, inventory standards, global supply chain considerations/outsourcing.

2. **Inputs/suppliers**
   Availability of suppliers, supplier concentration trends, nature of competition in the input or supplier industries, price trends, level of technology and important trends.

3. **Markets**
   Volume of sales in units and value in the industry, distribution channels, selling methods, consumer profile, nature of use of the products of the industry, trends in consumption. What are the products and services that meet the basic need?

4. **Human resources**
   Extent of unionization in the industry, union-management relations, availability of different classes of personnel, training practices.

5. **R&D and innovation**
   Nature of R&D in the industry, its importance, distribution of patents, rate of innovation and productivity.

6. **Finance**
   Sources of financing in the industry, difficulty in attracting capital.

Future Industry Trends

Limits on future growth of the industry, domestic and international competition, regulation.

Sources of Information

An increasing amount of information is available online. These include: Industry/environment information (World Bank, IMF, WTO, Europa World, Source OECD, STAT-USA, S&P NetAdvantage, etc.) and company data (D&B Key Business Ratios, Hoover's Online, Value Line, Mergent Online, EDGAR Search, Gale Virtual Reference Library, etc.).

OTHER SOURCES INCLUDE:

STANDARD & POOR'S COMPUSTAT

Forbes (mid-January issue)

Industry Norms and Key Business Ratios (by SIC codes)

Manufacturing USA: Industry Analyses, Statistics, and Leading Companies

Moody's Investors Fact Sheets: Industry Review

Predicasts F&S Indexes

Specific industry trade publications (e.g., *Beverage Industry, Computerworld, American Banker*)

Standard Industrial Classification Manual, Washington, D.C.

Ward's Business Directory of U.S. Private and Public Companies

Assessing Strategic Performance Through Financial Analysis

Managers must be comfortable with financial ratio analysis and what this information reveals, since ratios indicate the company's strength within its industry and the success of its strategic initiatives. In addition, investors look at company ratios in making decisions about whether to buy or sell stock and creditors use ratios to decide whether or not to lend money to a firm.

Although financial ratioss are used frequently as a measure of performance, some weaknesses with this method exist. The information provided is based on past data. While trends can be spotted, the information cannot be automatically applied to the future. In addition, the accuracy of the data assumes sound accounting procedures.

The four groups of financial/accounting ratios are profitability, leverage, liquidity, and activity.

Profitability

Profit ratios show how well the firm is being managed. Three ratios are particularly applicable to top management, and the larger the percentage, the better. The gross profit margin is useful in understanding the direct costs of the firm and how much is left to cover other expenses per dollar of sales.

Return on sales = Net profit/Total sales

Return on assets = Net profit/Total assets

Return on stockholders' equity = Net profit/Total stockholders' equity

Gross profit margin − Net sales − Cost of goods sold/Net sales

Leverage

Leverage ratios identify the source of a firm's capital. The sources are from owners (stockholders) or from external sources (outside creditors). As a general rule of thumb, lower debt ratios are preferred; however, the use of debt or the issuance of stock is typical in growth phases.

Debt ratio = Total debt/Total assets

Debt to equity ratio = Long-term debt/Total stockholders' equity

Activity

Activity ratios show how effectively a firm is using its resources. From a strategy perspective, asset turnover provides information as to how effectively a firm is generating sales from its asset base, and greater sales in relation to a firm's asset base is preferred (i.e., larger ratio).

Asset turnover = Total sales/Total assets

Liquidity

Liquidity ratios indicate whether a firm can meet its short-term obligations. Since slow-moving or obsolescent inventories can overstate the firm's ability to meet short-term obligations, the quick ratio removes these from the equation.

Current ratio = Current assets/Current liabilities

Quick ratio = Current assets – Inventories/Current liabilities

Assessing Strategic Performance Through Financial Analysis

Ratio Calculations Form

	Year T1	Year T2	Year T3
Net profit margin (return on sales) *Analysis:*	_____	_____	_____
Return on assets *Analysis:*	_____	_____	_____
Return on stockholders' equity *Analysis:*	_____	_____	_____
Gross profit margin *Analysis:*	_____	_____	_____
Asset turnover *Analysis:*	_____	_____	_____
Debt to assets *Analysis:*	_____	_____	_____
Debt to equity *Analysis:*	_____	_____	_____
Current ratio *Analysis:*	_____	_____	_____

Analysis: Briefly state what each ratio means using the numbers calculated. Complete the sentence, "For every $1.00 of (   ), there is $_____ of (   )."

Case Study 1

Strategic Alternatives at Mercury Telecom*

On a typically hot and humid summer day in central Texas, Dave Carter was on his way to take charge as the newly appointed CEO of Mercury Telecommunications. As he read the confidential white paper on Project Rusty, it became a bit clearer as to why he, an experienced turnaround executive, had been so aggressively recruited by a New York search firm for the job.

Mercury was a midsize, publicly traded telecommunications service provider with annual revenues approaching $1 billion. The company provided top-quality voice, data, IP, and transport services to corporations and other telecom companies and long distance services to households in certain geographic areas.

When he was first approached about the job by a new board member, Dave researched the company and found it to be in pretty fair shape. Because it was one of several service providers that owned its own network, the company had weathered the telecom storm in 2001–2004. However, once Dave was able to obtain more internal information and began to put the pieces together, the company's difficulties became clearer.

A careful analysis of the latest, yet-to-be-released income statement, balance sheet, and cash flow (see Exhibits) gave Dave the first clue. The company had lost money, but the cash balance was strong, primarily a result of a recent private placement of stock that yielded $160 million. The new investors were aware of the problems facing the company and had made their investment conditional to a change in leadership. Shortly after, Dave was contacted as part of a formal search for a new CEO. The current CEO, who was also the chairman, was a well-known fiber optics engineer who was well versed in equipment design, manufacturing, and engineering, but had little experience in the service business. As with most surviving telecom companies, Mercury had to grow; however, Dave knew from experience in Europe and the U.S. that the consumer business was subject to extreme pricing pressures and created a strain on customer service and engineering. He would look hard at this business line during his first 30 days.

Mercury had grown through a series of acquisitions, leaving it with a national presence and a good-sized network connecting big cities, but it lacked a deep network to reach the highly prized, high-volume business customers. However, even with the lack of a deep network with local reach, Mercury's sales and marketing staff had done a great job in attracting and retaining business customers. The downside to this was that Mercury had to buy this "reach" from other carriers, making its network costs very high. Dave realized this when he went over the numbers with his CFO that first week.

Mercury was aware of this growing problem, which brought Dave back to Project Rusty. It was a white paper written by his staff and bankers prior to his arrival that proposed the acquisition of VL Communications, a company that had the network "reach," but had not been successful with business customers. While it was an attractive

---

*Case prepared by Prof. Stephen Courter, McCombs School of Business, University of Texas at Austin, Austin, Texas, U.S., as a basis for class discussion and not to represent effective or ineffective management. The case describes a real situation with suitable changes to maintain confidentiality. We thank him for his contribution.

acquisition, the whisper price of over $1 billion was high relative to the company's earnings, and buying the firm would mean Mercury would have to go into debt—to the tune of $800 million—a thought that turned the new private placement (equity) investors red with anger. Two of the seven board members loved the deal to the point of stubbornness; most of the Mercury VP's also loved it since it would give them new responsibility after the close. But the current management team seemed to be spending more time pursuing this acquisition than running their departments. In any event, Dave had planned to bring a few executives with him, and he had already begun making calls to that end.

Dave knew about the conflicting stakeholder motivations, but the new investors, while vocal, only held 10% of the company's stock. In addition, VL had a very active investor who would hold firm on a price which was higher than that of comparable telecom companies. There was some question about this investor's willingness to even sell, placing some doubt in the bankers' minds as to the chances of a successful and rapid acquisition/closing. VL was a similar-sized company with weaker management, a less-than-sterling reputation, and a customer base that presented receivables problems, apparently due to quality issues.

Dave realized that Mercury needed more network assets to support the growth opportunity it enjoyed with its reputation with business customers. VL would get them that, but so would selling the consumer business and buying smaller regional networks. These two avenues, of course, were mutually exclusive. Building a new network would be too expensive, since landowners had a good sense of what their rights of way were worth; moreover, the capital markets were in no mood to fund new construction, having been burned in previous years with over capacity of fiber plant. Another route would be to selectively build a new network as new customers were signed up, but that presented a problem as to which should come first when it came to submitting bids.

Reviewing the balance sheet and income statement in light of the operational environment at Mercury, Dave knew he had to do something within six months or they would be back on the road looking for more cash. The operating losses, plus additional capital to support business customers and purchase network capacity (paid up front), showed a burn rate (i.e., cash usage) of $60–70 million a quarter. Additionally, the company was turning away good business daily since it couldn't provision the network solution efficiently. The revenue line showed good growth, but the cost of providing the service to business customers was about 20% higher than that of competitors.

Continuing his analysis of the company, Dave found more and more operational issues that were leading to the high costs. First, Sales was out of synch with Operations. Sales was selling services at a discounted price most of the time, and the price had been established by Marketing. Operations had no input at the time, so execs had little to no idea that their operational costs would not yield the margins for which Marketing was hoping. Moreover, Sales was selling a converged service of voice and data services that was designed to run on a single "black box" that the CTO and his staff had identified and cleared for use. Had the box worked with their network as theoretically designed, it would have yielded significant cost savings, almost enough to offset the higher line costs.

The former CEO, with his hardware background, loved the CTO's solution and had approved its implementation without extensive testing or a phased deployment. He turned Sales loose with it, and they, of course, sold it aggressively. It was touted as their competitive advantage—a simple, one box solution to provide a wide range of telecom services. It looked impressive on paper: it required less installation time, had fewer points of failure, included easy upgrades, and was less expensive for all parties.

Unfortunately, the new "black box" solution ran into problems that were aggravated with every new customer. In fact, to provide the promised level of service, a second box had to be put into use that increased both the capital and line costs for each customer. Dave came to a startling conclusion: the reason they were successful with the business customers was that they were providing a very expensive solution at a nominal price. Mercury was actually losing money on each service it was installing. This had to be fixed quickly; meanwhile, Sales would have to be reined in to stop selling the service, or to raise the price. Although it resulted in slower growth, the consumer business actually provided a positive impact to earnings that was, to a small extent, masking the problem from analysts.

Dave now fully understood why a key board member had pushed to bring in a new CEO, and a turnaround guy at that. The company looked all right at the top line, but was heading off a cliff. The new investors had put in enough money to give him time to find the problem and fix it before they ran out of cash.

After about four weeks, Dave had his first board meeting as the CEO. He gathered up his presentation and headed to the board room. They needed to hear his progress to date. Just before he left, his private line rang. Curious, Dave answered the phone himself and was surprised to hear the voice of Tim Palmer on the line.

Tim was also a seasoned telecom CEO who had been running Gunite Telecom, a larger competitor to Mercury, for many years. Dave's and Tim's paths had crossed amicably over the past 10 years. In fact Tim had tried, unsuccessfully, to buy both of Dave's previous companies.

"Dave, what are you doing back in telecom?" Tim bellowed in a friendly voice. "I thought you were teaching back East somewhere!"

"I was, but this was a terrific opportunity to run a company on the verge of great growth," Dave answered.

"That just means you're going after my customers and market share!" Tim said.

"Exactly," Dave responded. "I just closed on a house here, and the moving truck delivers our stuff tomorrow."

"Guess the only way to stop you is to buy you guys now before you make it even more valuable. You guys have great products, but you know I've got a bigger network!"

This time there was a seriousness in Tim's voice that Dave had heard before.

"Okay, but remember what's happened in the past. If you want us, bid high, and bid a lot of cash! No restrictions on stock!" Dave said.

"Message received!" Tim answered." Talk to you soon."

Dave hung up and stood by the phone, wondering if this was relevant to share with the board at this stage. Meanwhile, his assistant came in and said the board was waiting.

MERCURY
UNAUDITED CONDENSED CONSOLIDATED BALANCE SHEETS
(in thousands, except share and per share amounts)

	December 31, 2005	March 31, 2006
ASSETS		
Current assets:	$	$
Cash and cash equivalents	66,706	157,251
Short-term investments	42,648	16,985
Trade accounts receivable, net allowances of $36,977 and $37,412 at December 31, 2005 and March 31, 2006, respectively	75,579	73,867
Prepaids and other current assets	18,565	23,629
Total current assets	203,498	271,732
Restricted cash, non-current	14,606	14,060
Property and equipment, net	260,681	261,268
Goodwill	58,354	58,354
Intangible assets, net	24,820	23,416
Other non-current assets, net	11,545	24,957
Total assets	573,504	653,787
LIABILITIES AND STOCKHOLDERS' EQUITY		
Current liabilities:	$	$
Notes payable, net of discounts, and capital lease obligations, current portion	33,072	1,663
Accounts payable	32,221	48,640
Accrued expenses and other liabilities	54,344	51,354
Accrued communication service costs	25,441	17,104
Deferred revenue, current portion	6,941	6,718
Accrued restructuring and other charges	3,965	4,492
Total current liabilities	155,984	129,971
Notes payable, net of discounts, and capital lease obligations, current portion	20,819	20,382
Deferred revenue, current portion	17,939	17,639
Other long-term liabilities	13,750	12,317
Total liabilities	208,492	180,309
COMMITMENTS AND CONTINGENCIES		
Stockholders' equity:	$	$
Common stock—$0.01 par value, 1,900,000,000 shares authorized; 75,266,437 shares issued and 74,038257 shares outstanding as of December 31, 2005; 88,082,830 shares issued and 87,155,664 shares outstanding as of March 31, 2006	747	876
Treasury Stock (1,228,180 shares December 31, 2005 and March 31, 2006, at cost)	(9,512)	(9,512)
Additional paid-in capital	3,180,764	3,308,876
Accumulated other comprehensive loss:		
Unrealizable investment losses	(220)	(36)
Accumulated deficit	(2,806,767)	(2,826,726)
Total stockholders' equity	365,012	473,478
Total liabilities and stockholders' equity	573,504	653,787

MERCURY
UNAUDITED CONDENSED CONSOLIDATED STATEMENTS OF OPERATIONS
(In thousands, expect per share amounts)

	Three Months Ended	
	March 31, 2005	March 31, 2006
	$	$
Revenue	218,255	224,046
Cost of Revenue (excluding depreciation expense of $21,553 and $12,653 for the period ending March 31, 2005 and 2006, respectively)	147,623	143,721
Research and development (including equity-based compensation expense of $318 and $0 for the period ended March 31, 2005 and 2006, respectively)	2,883	—
Sales, general, and administrative (including equity-based compensation expense of $632 and $1,803 for the period ended March 31, 2005 and 2006, respectively)	74,427	79,861
Litigation settlement	2,000	—
Depreciation	26,471	15,444
Amortization	1,418	1,404
Restructuring, severance, and gain on sale of fixed assets (including equity-based compensation expense of $0 and $2,364 for the period ended March 31, 2005 and 2006, respectively)	(313)	2,631
Total operating expense	254,509	243,061
Operating loss	(36,254)	(9,015)
Other income, net	1,952	1,336
Interest expense, net of capitalized amounts	(9,163)	(2,280)
Net loss	(43,465)	(19,959)
Unrealized investment loss	(156)	(36)
Comprehensive loss	(43,621)	(19,995)
Basic and diluted net loss per common share	(0.62)	(0.26)
Basic and diluted weighted average common shares	70,398	77,169

MERCURY
UNAUDITED CONDENSED CONSOLIDATED STATEMENTS OF CASH FLOW
(in thousands)

	Three Months Ended	
	March 31, 2005	March 31, 2006
Cash flows from operating activities:		
Net loss	(43,465)	(19,959)
Adjustments to reconcile net loss to net cash used in operating activities:		
Depreciation and amortization	27,890	16,849
Equity-based compensation expense	950	1,803
Provision for bad debt and sales allowances	7,462	8,694
Deferred financing, original issue discount amortization, and accretion of interest	7,713	1,368
Amortization of deferred revenue and other	1,253	(380)
Non-cash restructing, severance, and gain on sale of fixed assets	(497)	94
Changes in operating assets and liabilities, excluding acquired amounts:		
Account receivable	(10,796)	(6,982)
Other current assets	(5,229)	(9,914)
Account payable and other accrued expenses	(8,734)	4,265
Net cash used in operating activities	(23,453)	(4,163)
Cash flows from investing activities:		
Purchase of property and equipment	(13,452)	3,746)
Ciena equipment deposit	—	(11,000)
Proceeds from the sale of property and equipment	232	2,761
Purchase of investments	(40,864)	(6,057)
Sales of investments	38,039	31,904
Net cash provided by (used in) investing activities	(16,046)	3,859
Cash flows from financing activities:		
Proceeds from private placements of common stock, net of issuance cost of $6 million	—	103,975
Proceeds from stock options and warrants exercised	656	2,899
(Increase) decrease in deposits and other non-current assets	(613)	546
Repayment of notes payable and capital lease obligations	(385)	(16,572)
Net cash provided by (used in) financing activities	(342)	90,849
Net increase (decrease) in cash and cash equivalents	(39,841)	90,545
Cash and cash equivalents—beginning of period	124,540	66,706
Cash and cash equivalents—end of period	84,699	157,251
Supplemental disclosure of cash flow information:		
Interest paid	672	221
Supplemental disclosure of noncash activities:		
Repayment of convertible notes with common stock	34,168	16,072
Deposit with Ciena converted to equipment	—	2,136

Case Study 2

Caffeine Satisfaction: Rivalry Among the Coffee Shops

Coffee was one of the oldest products known to mankind and was consumed around the world as a stimulant. In traded commodities, it was second only to oil. The consumer often developed a personal relationship with this product and had strong preferences in taste and brewing methods. Yet, retailing standardized cups of coffee was big business that led to strong rivalry. This case provides an overview of the industry and describes the efforts of Dunkin' Donuts and Starbucks, two companies that followed their separate paths towards satisfying consumer needs.

The Industry

Coffee consumption can be traced back to before 1000 C.E. in Ethiopia. Arab traders were credited with bringing the *coffea arabica* plant to the Middle East for cultivation. Coffee consumption reached Europe in the 1600s and an early coffee house, where merchants gathered, existed in London in 1668. This shop eventually became Lloyd's, the insurance headquarters. An alternative to Arabica was Robusta (*coffea canephora*), a hardy strain of coffee that yielded double the beans per acre. It produced a harsh and bitter taste when brewed and large manufacturers often blended the Arabica with Robusta beans to produce lower-cost blends. Currently, about 75% of coffee production in the world is Arabica, with the rest being Robusta and other minor strains. Sometimes, especially in preparation of instant coffee, chicory, a plant with a deep tap root, was added.

Over the period 2003–2008, Brazil, Colombia, and Vietnam topped the list as producers and exporters out of about 45 countries that produced coffee. Brazil had for long been the major source of premium Arabica beans. Central America and Vietnam were also mass suppliers of coffee, and the latter was prominent mainly in the last 10 years as a supplier of lower quality beans. The nature of the coffee market and its distribution resulted in the cost of coffee beans making up only about 10% of the end-user price in the United States. No matter how coffee demand grew, the farmer appeared to get little of the benefits.

The International Coffee Organization (ICO) (**www.ico.org**) was founded in 1963 under the auspices of the United Nations because of the great economic importance of coffee. It aimed to bring together producing and consuming countries to deal with the challenges facing the world coffee sector through international cooperation. Its members included coffee exporting and importing countries and it administered agreements that attempted to produce fair trade. ICO exporting members accounted for over 97% of world coffee production and its importing members were responsible for 68% of world coffee consumption. The consumer concern about poor working conditions, use of child labor, and subsistence wages paid to farmers who grew the coffee led to several movements in the developed countries to promote "ethical" coffee. Under various banners such as "Equal Exchange" (**www.equalexchange.com**), "Fair Trade Coffee" (**www.fairtradecoffee.org**), and the Utz Kapeh Foundation (**www.utzcertified.org**), the fair trade organizations dealt with cooperatives of small farmers who were guaranteed a contract price, and ensured that farms adhered to a code that included fair wages, healthcare for workers, and curbed waste and pollution.

Global coffee demand has maintained a slow growth of 2% to 4% in recent years. Producer countries account for about 26% of the consumption and importers about 74%.

The market among importers, mostly developed countries, tends toward saturation with slow or negative growth. Consumption among the producer countries has grown faster, both due to population and economic growth. Most consumption (about 58%) has taken place in mature markets of the European Union, the United States, and Japan. However, the fastest growth in consumption was in the Asia-Pacific region and in Central and Eastern Europe.

Coffee prices over the recent past reversed their previous falling trend. Composite prices (i.e., over different varieties), from a high of $6 per pound in 1977, fell to about $1.71 in 1986, and averaged 48 cents in 2001. It since recovered to $1.04 in 2007, the highest since 1995–1996. These prices were still low considering cost of production leading to economic and other problems in the farming sector of various countries.

Americans used to be known for their heavy consumption of coffee. For long, coffee consumption was the number one beverage in the United States after tap water. However, average consumption per head, which was at a peak of 3.1 cups per day in 1963, was less than 2 cups by late 1980s and continued to fall due to the availability of several alternatives (Table 1). The rest of the world drank more tea than anything else besides water. The way people drank coffee also changed over the years. A kind of generic coffee was typically available in all convenience stores, gas stations, restaurants, and the like. However, more and more consumers became conscious of what beans were used and how much "delicacy" was put into brewing their cup of coffee. They were also willing to pay more money to get a premium coffee latte or mocha. Within coffee consumption, the distribution of regular and premium (i.e., 25% above value brands) coffee had also undergone a change (Table 2). Between 2000 and 2006, premium (or gourmet) had risen from 12% to 17% of total coffee consumed.

TABLE 1   U.S. BEVERAGE CONSUMPTION (GALLONS PER CAPITA PER YEAR)

Year	Tea	Coffee	Bottled Water	Fruit Drinks	Vegetable Juices	Soft Drinks	Total
1980	7.3	19.2	2.7	7.6	24.3	n/a	61.0
1990	6.9	19.4	8.8	18.9	23.9	47.1	125.0
2000	8.3	20.0	16.7	23.8	21.7	53.2	143.9
2001	8.7	18.5	18.2	23.9	21.8	52.9	143.9
2002	8.3	20.1	20.1	22.7	21.8	52.8	143.8
2003	8.0	18.5	21.6	23.1	21.6	52.4	145.2
2004	8.4	18.8	23.2	22.9	21.6	52.3	147.2
2005	8.4	18.5	25.4	22.1	21.3	51.5	147.3

Note: Soft drinks includes diet and regular; tea includes bottle/canned iced tea; fruit drinks includes juices, drinks, cocktails and ades.
Source: U.S. Department of Agriculture Tables, March 2007.

Coffee shops that also sell snacks and bakery products competed with doughnut shops, bakeries, supermarket bakeries, gourmet cookie shops, restaurants, convenience stores, and even ice cream franchises such as Dairy Queen. Although fast food restaurants were not direct competitors, chains such as McDonald's offering breakfast saw the potential in this market. Doughnuts were a major sales item in supermarket bakeries. Convenience stores also moved into food service at a rapid rate. They also served coffee, sold packaged doughnuts, were open long hours and were in premium locations.

Various trends, apart from changes in consumer tastes, impacted coffee consumption. Public libraries in the United States were increasingly allowing their patrons to bring drinks to the premises in response to the competition they faced from bookstores that had coffee bars. Medical research revealed positive and negative benefits from drinking coffee. An example of a positive impact was the link between high coffee consumption (seven cups a day) and a lower risk of developing type-2 diabetes. In doses of 200 milligrams or less, the caffeine, a mild central nervous system stimulant, produced feelings of alertness and sociability. However, other studies found that it could raise blood pressure, and some

TABLE 2 U.S. COFFEE CONSUMPTION

	Cups per Capita per Day		
Year	Regular	Gourmet	Total
1960	2.77	NA	2.77
1970	2.57	NA	2.57
1980	2.02	NA	2.02
1990	1.71	NA	1.71
2000	1.45	0.20	1.65
2001	1.39	0.33	1.72
2002	1.31	0.33	1.64
2003	1.24	0.26	1.50
2004	1.23	0.41	1.64
2005	1.39	0.36	1.75
2006	1.56	0.33	1.89

Note: Regular includes decaffeinated. Figures are approximate and have been recalculated from the original.
Source: U.S. Department of Agriculture Tables, June 2006.

doctors recommended against it for pregnant women, or those with insomnia or heartburn. There was also concern that high doses of caffeine may result in a physical dependency and produce withdrawal symptoms such as headaches and poor concentration.

The United States accounted for 25% of global coffee imports. Specialty (also called gourmet or premium) coffee beverages accounted for about 40% of the $35 billion US coffee market. Average price of specialty beans was twice that of traditional coffee. While it was a high margin segment and known to set trends, it also showed signs of maturing.

Under tough economic conditions in the U.S., consumers usually placed a lot of importance on price and perceived value. Among beverages, although carbonated soft drinks showed sluggish growth, noncarbonated drinks showed an ability to attract customers. Most U.S. producers of food, beverages, and related products were small and the industry was fragmented although a few major companies were dominant and operated worldwide. As the dollar weakened against the euro and other currencies, it had a positive effect on companies with significant sales overseas while it made imports of commodities, such as coffee, more expensive.

Dunkin' Donuts

Dunkin' Donuts shops sold coffee beverages—as well as well-known bakery products such as doughnuts, muffins, cookies, bagels, and also sandwiches. They had a reputation for freshness and consistency of their products, apart from convenient locations. The stores were designed for easy access and quick service, while some had televisions tuned to news channels, and also a drive-through window.

The chain was founded by Bill Rosenberg, who opened his first doughnut shop in 1948 in Quincy, Massachusetts and named it Open Kettle. Two years later the company became Dunkin' Donuts. In 1968, Rosenberg went public and the company started an aggressive expansion both nationally and abroad. It opened its first overseas shop in Japan in 1970. By 2003, it operated over 5,500 stores worldwide, of which about 4,000 were in the United States. The overseas locations in 30 countries included significant presence in the Philippines, Indonesia, South Korea, and Thailand.

In 1989, the company was acquired by British beverage giant, Allied Domecq PLC. This venture impacted Dunkin' Donuts' strategy in various ways as it became part of a major corporation. Allied Domecq began co-branding Dunkin' Donuts with its other businesses, namely Togo's Eatery (a deli-style sandwich shop) and Baskin Robbins, an ice cream chain. Company officials found that combining the businesses in one location generated business through the day. By 2003, the company had about 600 such co-branded stores. All the brands under Dunkin' Donuts roof primarily served customers on the go. Some stores provided a few tables for those customers who liked to enjoy their breakfast or lunch on the premises, but this was not universal, especially in small and crowded downtown shops.

Dunkin' Donuts' main expansion strategy was through franchising, which it began to do in 1955 when the concept of franchising was itself in its early stages. Dunkin' Donuts required potential franchisees to have a proven track record in successfully managing a small- to medium- sized business; experience in hiring, training, and motivating employees; sound understanding of business finance principles; and strong personal commitment to managing franchised stores on a daily basis. Franchisees paid about 5.9% of total sales as royalty fees and could expect a 20% to 25% return on investment.

The franchising system followed different approaches. In some cases the franchisee owned the site and in other cases, the company acquired appropriate sites and leased it to the franchisee. The company's rental income from company-owned sites was a significant revenue stream even when compared to franchisee royalty payments. Franchise agreements, initially, granted the franchisee the right to operate at a specified location without territorial exclusivity. Since 1990, the company gave territorial rights, too. The company carefully screened potential new locations to ensure optimal penetration. Disputes, however, arose between the company and its franchisees not only about cannibalization potential from new outlets, but also with regard to operational matters such as following company policies regarding cleanliness, maintenance of records, and the like. Some disputes ended up in court. Over time, the company moved away from a system of individual franchisee to awarding regional store development rights in new markets.

Dunkin' Donuts also entered into alliances with grocery retail chains such as Stop & Shop Supermarkets and Shaw's, in which selected supermarkets feature a Dunkin' Donuts store on the premises. Nevertheless, Dunkin' Donuts was slow in achieving a nationwide presence in the United States, partly due to an inability to find appropriate franchisees. About two-thirds of its stores were located in the northeast and mid-Atlantic states. Sales pattern varied between regions. Northeastern outlets were primarily coffee shops as against the rest of the country where doughnuts were the profit generator.

A Dunkin' Donuts outlet initially manufactured the products it sold. Franchisees received extensive training at Dunkin' Donuts University, and were prepared to manage the front office retail and the back office production. Initially there were three production shifts to maintain the required freshness of products. Staffing problems made this difficult for some franchisees, and the company responded through research and development efforts that extended the shelf life of the products so they stayed fresher longer with two-shift production. The company also built central production centers for donuts and other baked items. Franchisees were required to buy delivery trucks and collect the baked goods three times a day. This enabled franchisees to save on real estate costs because stores would require about 2,000 sq. ft. less space without the need for baking equipment on premises.

Since many shops operated on a 24-hour basis, finding reliable employees for managing the production and sales was often a problem. A significant number of franchisees were immigrants from countries such as Pakistan, Morocco, Portugal, and India who were prepared to work long hours. They also often employed relatives to ease the supervisory or operational problems. The company designed programs to help franchisees improve operations. To improve speed of service and maintain quality, the operating system was made team-based. Rather than each person doing different duties, from taking the order, filling it, and ringing up the bill, the new system changed to be team based with individuals doing a particular job. Contests were also initiated between shops with winning teams given cash awards. Franchisees bought their supplies through a cooperative formed by them for the purpose of better bargaining power. There were five such co-ops in the United States.

The company purchased its coffee beans from three countries in Central and South America. Suppliers had to adhere to stringent bean-growing guidelines. The company also sampled and blended its coffee much as a vintner cultivates wine to achieve the Dunkin' Donuts coffee taste.

Franchisees contributed 5% of gross sales to an advertising and promotion fund. Due to an uneven distribution of stores around the United States, the company used regional instead of national television and radio advertising. Costs of new promotions were borne entirely by the franchisees and they could choose to participate or not.

While pursuing innovation in its product offerings, the company also successfully imitated the new products of others. After Starbucks launched its Frappuccino, Dunkin' Donuts came out with its successful Coolatta. When bagels became popular in the country, the company responded to an initiative by a franchisee to include fresh bagels in their product mix and the company eventually became the largest bagel retailer in the United States. Its introduction of espresso and latte was an attempt to provide pricier drinks for the mainstream customer. It even promised to serve the cappuccino in less than a minute. Ken Kimmel, a vice president of the chain's marketing arm said, "We watch trends and then Dunkinize them."

While trained baristas at Starbucks took about a minute and a half to prepare a cappuccino for sale at about $3.35, a customer would get it for about $2.90 at half the time in a Dunkin' Donuts (see Table 3 for a price comparison). To achieve that, the company bought automated pushbutton machines that ground the beans, added the right amount of hot water and, using a sensor, steamed the milk to the right temperature. A separate machine dispensed the right amount of milk. The coffee and the milk were then manually combined for some visual effect.

TABLE 3   COMPARISON OF PRICES (US$ PER CUP) — DUNKIN' DONUTS AND STARBUCKS

	Dunkin' Donuts			Starbucks		
	Small	Medium	Large	Small	Medium	Large
Regular	1.55	1.85	1.99	1.65	1.85	1.95
Lattes/Cappuccinos	2.49	2.89	3.09	2.80	3.35	3.65
Flavored/Specialty drinks	2.79	3.79	4.49	3.10–3.50	3.65–4.00	3.95–4.50

Note: Prices are indicative and may vary between regions.

In 2005, the French beverage company Pernod-Ricard acquired Allied Domecq and, pursuant to that, Dunkin' Donuts, Baskin Robbins, and Togo Restaurants were sold to a group of private investors in the U.S. the next year. They named the group Dunkin' Brands Inc. (Togo was subsequently divested by the investors.) The private company does not publish financial performance data. Various news reports suggested sales revenues of about $3.4 billion in 2004, $3.85 billion in 2005, and $4.7 billion for 2006 (in worldwide system sales, according to the company's Web site). Coffee was the major product for Dunkin' Donuts, and accounted for about 50% of its sales. Doughnuts contributed about 20% and the remaining came from breakfast foods such as muffins, bagels, and sandwiches.

Jon Luther, who was appointed CEO of Allied Domecq's quick-service restaurants in February 2003, continued under the new ownership. He viewed Starbucks as the primary competition. His initiatives included changes in the menu, store redesign, and a big push on new franchises. While menu development was previously under the marketing department, he created a separate unit for this. The company also planned to expand more aggressively in the southern and western regions of the United States. Newer products such as hot sandwiches were being aimed at reducing dependence on doughnuts, offering a healthier fare, and spreading demand more evenly through the day. In October 2003, the company pushed into the specialty coffee segment and launched a new line of espresso-based products such as latte and cappuccino.

With new capital infusion after going private, the company pursued its growth with new products and multiple formats. The company saw itself as the "quick quality" leader in the industry, offering a quick dining experience through innovative products, served fresh, and meeting the needs of busy people. It planned to grow the brands nationally and internationally. In 2008, it reported 7,200 stores (owned and franchised), of which 5,300 stores were in 34 states of the U.S. and 1,900 in 30 countries. The company planned to rely on multiple formats (stores, gas stations, carts, etc.) to reach 15,000 locations in the U.S. by 2020.

The company added yogurt drinks and iced tea to its portfolio of beverages and saw these as growth items. The company, which established itself as serving simple fare to working-class customers, had to walk a fine line between adding style and not appearing pretentious, something its loyal customers disliked. Their hot sandwiches were referred to as anytime breakfast sandwiches, as customers felt that the original name "panini" was too fancy. They introduced music in some stores, but when they tried to paint the stores in coffee-colored hues, customers made them go back to the bright pink they always used. The company conducted psychographic studies to gauge people's values and attitudes to determine new locations as they executed their expansion plans.

Dunkin' Donuts also expanded into nontraditional venues such as colleges, hospitals, and stadiums. The company entered into an arrangement with Proctor & Gamble to distribute its packaged coffee to grocery stores, club stores and other retail outlets. It also entered into arrangements with Sara Lee, the food products company, to sell coffee in office buildings and private cafeterias, and with Hess gas stations to dispense it through drink kiosks. In 2008, franchisees in the northeast U.S. protested these aggressive growth moves saying they cut into franchisee sales and profits.

Starbucks

Starbucks (www.starbucks.com) was founded in Seattle, Washington, in 1971 by coffee aficionados Gordon Bowker, Jerry Baldwin, and Ziv Siegl. The shop only sold premium high-grade Arabica beans roasted to a dark extreme by a professional—and perfectionist—roaster. In 1982, the company, which had grown to five stores, hired Howard Schultz to manage its retail sales and marketing. On a trip to Italy, Schultz was captivated by the culture of coffee and the romance of the coffee bars in Milan. With the owners reluctant to go in that direction, he left the company and started his own coffee bar in Chicago selling a coffee brand called Starbucks. In 1987, he bought the Starbucks stores from the owners and combined them with his own to form the Starbucks Corporation with 11 stores. (The company went public in 1992.) Starbucks was on its way to becoming a major retailer of coffee beverages. In 1988, it introduced a mail-order catalog and by the end of the year was serving customers in every state. The catalog helped build awareness as well as point the company to potential locations for its cafés. For many years, the company spent little on advertising, relying instead on word of mouth to build a reputation.

Starbucks subsequently grew into a premium coffee empire that featured a coffee shop where you not only drank the best coffee in town, but also relaxed and socialized. The company built consumer loyalty through its superior dark roast coffee, customized espresso drinks, responsive customer service, and an appealing store experience. Stores featured comfortable seating and soft music. The company realized the importance of educating the consumers in order to build a market for specialty coffee. This involved employees communicating their knowledge of, and enthusiasm for, coffee. Starbucks specialty coffee shops served a variety of coffees and coffee drinks. In addition, they also sold teas, pastries and other food items, espresso machines, coffee brewers, and assorted items such as thermal coffee cups with the Starbucks logo.

The company appealed to a target audience of 25 to 45 years of age and generated about 50% of its revenue between 7:00 A.M. and 10:00 A.M. Some of its growth resulted from extending beyond the traditional coffee drink. In 1999, the company experimented with prepackaged sandwiches (to appeal to lunchtime customers), but found people preferred pastries instead. Creative extensions of coffee with different flavors resulted in the chain selling more than 30 distinct drinks.

Schultz said he subscribed to a philosophy of "hire people smarter than you are and get out of their way." From the beginning, he recruited experts in the areas of finance, human resources, marketing, and mail-order in his senior management. In the middle ranks, experienced managers were hired from Taco Bell, Wendy's, and Blockbuster.

The company installed an expensive computer network and designed a point-of sale system, via PCs, for managers to use. The sales information from every store was passed on to the headquarters every night allowing analysis to identify regional buying trends quickly.

The company adopted creditable policies for treating the employees well. In 1991, it became the first privately owned company to offer an employee stock ownership program that included part-time employees. Health and dental benefits were also offered to both full- and part-timers. These innovations helped achieve a low rate of turnover. Employee training included 25 hours of coursework about the history of coffee, drink preparation, and how to brew a perfect cup. The company believed that committed and enthusiastic employees were more likely to deliver good service and provide an inviting environment for customers.

In the late 1980s and early 1990s, the company invested substantial time and efforts into building accounting, planning, and logistics systems in preparation for rapid growth—and did not make profits between 1987 and 1989. However, venture capitalists, attracted by the 20% growth of the specialty coffee market, came forward with funds.

Rather than buy from wholesalers, the company bought its coffee beans directly from producing countries and executives traveled around the world to meet with farmers and get acquainted with all aspects of the commodity business. The beans were then roasted and blended by trained personnel before being shipped to the outlets. As a measure of quality control, once a bag was opened, the beans had to be used within seven days or donated to charity. Roasters were trained for more than a year before being allowed to roast a batch. Facing allegations from a human rights group that the company was buying beans from wholesalers who were paying poverty wages, Starbucks began to buy more coffee certified as "fair trade."

The company operated its own stores and had an in-house team of architects, real estate personnel, and construction managers to find the right locations and create the right structure. In congested downtown districts, kiosks were opened. The company first opened in a major market that served as a logistical and managerial base or hub to enable further expansion in that region. An important part of its store expansion strategy was "store clustering," when Starbucks opened several stores close to each other to attract consumer attention, gain market share, and prevent other coffee retailers from entering the area.

The company experienced rapid growth in sales in the early years. For instance, sales growth was 65% per year from 1990–1993. By 1997, it had reached 1,412 stores and sales reached $1 billion. The rapid growth of the company and intensive geographic coverage even resulted in protests in cities such as Toronto, San Francisco, and Portland, with local citizens supporting local businesses and wanting to keep the chain out of their neighborhood. The company also made horizontal acquisitions to strengthen market position. It purchased the Coffee Connection, a 23-store rival based in Boston for $23 million in 1994, making it a wholly owned subsidiary.

The first overseas venture came in 1996, in Japan, through a joint venture with a prominent local retailer, Sazaby, Inc. Similar ventures with local partners were entered into in Hawaii, Singapore, and the Philippines. In foreign countries, the company conducted focus groups, and sent its foreign managers back to Seattle for 13 weeks of training. It employed a high degree of cultural sensitivity in setting up its new foreign operations.

When Starbucks expanded into the United Kingdom in 1998, it acquired Seattle Coffee Company, a specialty coffee firm and converted its units to the Starbucks name. The company's overseas expansion into 30 countries beyond the United States and Canada, while aggressive, did not meet the same success as in North America. In June 2003, 1,532 stores overseas accounted for 23% of the total number of stores, but only 9% of the sales revenues. The company lost money in Japan and Britain, restructured operations, and closed stores in Europe and the Middle East. In some countries, it acquired licensed operations or increased its equity position over time. The problems in overseas operations arose from high startup costs, local competition on price, and the different expectations of store experience.

Some ventures took the company into different business areas. The company opened a full-service casual restaurant called Café Starbucks and, in 1999, acquired the Pasqua Coffee Co., which owned a chain of coffee and sandwich shops in New York and

California. Although Starbucks had developed its own in-house tea brand Infusia, it also acquired Tazo Tea Company in 1999.

The company entered the music business indirectly when it began selling CDs in its stores in the mid-80s. Schultz saw music and entertainment as helping to draw customers. It acquired a five-store Hear Music Chain in San Francisco in 1999. It helped produce CDs and even offered some exclusive music in its stores, and media bars allowed customers to burn their own CDs. Analysts did not believe that music would account for more than 2% of retail store sales.

The company started a series of partnerships with different businesses such as United Airlines, Host Marriott, Nordstrom's, and Barnes & Noble to open kiosks or facilitate bulk sales of its beverage. It also acquired different players, especially in the international arena. The company entered into a joint venture with PepsiCo to bottle Frappuccino beverages for sale through supermarkets and convenience stores. A joint venture with Dreyer's Grand Ice Cream involved the development and sales of Starbucks Ice Cream. Within a year, it became the number one coffee ice cream in the United States. Starbucks also signed a long-term licensing arrangement with Kraft Foods for the marketing and distribution of Starbucks whole bean and ground coffee in grocery, warehouse club, and mass-merchandise stores. These partnerships and the wholesale business further helped build brand awareness. The company also sold wholesale its coffee to restaurants, businesses, educational institutions, hospitals, hotels, and airlines.

Starbucks launched a Web site with an online store in 1998, and Schultz reportedly wanted Starbucks to ultimately sell everything from gourmet foods to furniture, although some of these plans were subsequently scaled back. The company also attempted a failed acquisition of Williams Sonoma, Inc., a retailer of high-end kitchenware. Some analysts questioned the wisdom of a company that was moving so far from its core business. In mid-1999, the stock fell 28% following announcement of a shortfall in earnings making the company pull back from its Internet-sales plans. Nevertheless, the company provided high-speed Internet connections in its stores to encourage people to stay and compete against Internet and cybercafés. In 2000, Schultz stepped down from the CEO position and became chief global strategist.

The new CEO introduced several changes in its format. It began selling hot sandwiches, added drive-through windows, and switched to automatic espresso machines to improve on speed of service and efficiency. In pursuit of growth, the company opened 3,000 new stores in just the two years between 2005 and 2007. Table 4 gives the distribution of the company's stores. Although Starbucks had a preference for company-owned stores, which generated 85% of 2007 sales, licensing and franchise allowed it to expand to 35 countries.

TABLE 4   GEOGRAPHIC DISTRIBUTION OF STORES, 2007

Location	Company	License/Franchise	Total
United States	6793	3891	10,684
International	1712	2615	4,327
Total	8505	2615	15,011

Source: Hoover's Company Profile, 2008.

The company's 2007 revenues of $9.4 billion was almost three times the figure of 2002 ($3.3 billion) and a compound annual growth rate of 23% over five years. The sales mix by product type was 75% beverages, 17% food items, 3% whole bean coffees, and 5% coffee-related hardware items. Yet, the company began to face a slowdown, with some store sales rising just 1% by early 2008. The stock price fell by nearly 50% in 2007; analysts believed that the firm's troubles arose from both overexpansion and the rising commodity prices that had driven two price increases in the chain. In early 2007, Chairman Howard Schultz wondered, in a memo to all employees, if the company was becoming more like a fast food chain and losing the "romance and theater" of its stores.

In response, Schultz again assumed the CEO position in early 2008. The company scaled down its expansion plans of eventually having 40,000 stores, and said it planned 2,000 new stores in 2008. Among some new steps initiated was the decision to stop selling hot sandwiches (that was tried for two years), because it felt that the food smell interfered with the aroma of coffee and made the store look like a fast-food chain. The company also began experimenting with a $1 coffee. Table 5 summarizes Starbucks' five-year performance.

TABLE 5 FIVE-YEAR SALES/NET INCOME (IN U.S. DOLLARS)

Year	Sales ($ millions)	Net Income ($ millions)
2007	9,411.5	672.6
2006	7,786.9	581.5
2005	6,369.3	494.5
2004	5,294.3	390.6
2003	4075.5	268.3

Other Players

The coffee retailing industry covered a range from mom-and-pop stores to national chains. Various players devised their own unique strategies to compete in the market.

A few years ago, Krispy Kreme Doughnuts, Inc., a North Carolina-based company, seemed to be a potential challenger in this market. It sold mainly doughnuts, based on a secret recipe—and coffee. Its famous hot glazed doughnuts attracted a loyal following and helped build the company's reputation. Its full-sized outlets were like factories, with costly doughnut-making machinery that customers could see behind a glass churning out more than the store could sell, which were sold through area grocery stores. Krispy Kreme expanded through its own stores and gave rights to franchisees to develop major markets. However, accounting irregularities and conflicts of interests issues led to losses in 2006 and slowed down growth. It had over 300 stores in the U.S.

McDonald's Corp., which saw rivals draw away its customers by offering sandwiches, also decided to enter the specialty coffee segment. By end 2008, it opened coffee bars selling McCafe drinks (lattes and cappuccinos, apart from regular drip coffee) inside 3000 of its nearly 14,000 stores in the U.S.. It priced these drinks to be less expensive than Dunkin Donuts and Starbucks and expected them to add between 5% and 10% to store sales. Peet's Coffee & Tea Inc., a specialty-coffee company that mainly sold coffee beans through grocery stores, had about 168 stores and planned to open more, especially in major East Coast markets. Tim Hortons, a Canadian doughnuts and coffee retailer similar to Dunkin Donuts with 2,711 stores and 76% share of the market in Canada (in 2007), operated about 340 stores in towns near the U.S.–Canada border. The company planned to increase its stores in U.S. markets, especially in the New England region. Minneapolis-based Caribou Coffee, with 480 stores in 18 states, was also looking for growth and had launched a premium iced-coffee line.

Conclusion

The coffee retailing industry in the U.S. was going through a period of transition. Observers wondered if it had reached saturation and whether the coffee category was commoditizing. At the same time, while Starbucks and Dunkin' Donuts battled for a share of the consumers' caffeine intake, some wondered if these companies were really rivals. Morningstar analyst Carl Sibiski observed, "There's a lot of professionals running around here in downtown Chicago who pass up Starbucks and go to Dunkin' Donuts. They really have two different brands and their brands mean different things." When Howard Schultz was asked (in 2004) what the difference was between Dunkin' and Starbucks, he responded, "We are in the business of creating an experience in our stores that goes beyond the product. The product is not just the coffee, it's the relationship we have with our customers, the environment, the music, the entire setting." Yet, along with continued growth, the focus of these companies was on how to innovate and respond to consumer's coffee needs, even as they faced constant challenge from newcomers.

Team Projects   161

MICA Method of Case Analysis and
Discussion   163

PART V

Semester Projects

Team Projects

Project A: Comparing Two Organizations in the Same Industry

Project B: Identifying Strategic Issues at Local Business Organizations

> **OBJECTIVES**
>
> These guidelines for two team projects help prepare you and your team for studying strategic issues that organizations face in the context of their environment.

A model of strategic management stipulates that there be a fit between the firm and its environment in order for the firm to achieve its long-term goals. Both of the projects described below provide a framework for analyzing the strategy of a firm in relation to its environment. Teams that work on Project A will compare and contrast the strategic issues faced by two competitors in the same industry. If access to a local organization is possible, Project B is another option that gives teams an opportunity to analyze the strategic management process and its various components at a nearby firm.

Teams should comprise three to five learners. Each project is divided into phases as described in the left column of its respective table. In the right column, relevant Strategy Sessions or industry profiles have been suggested for the teams to review that provide examples of how to apply analytical models to company situations.

Project A: Comparing Two Organizations in the Same Industry

Phase I Industry Analysis	Strategy Sessions/Industry Profile
1. Choose an industry.	See Part IV – Lodging Industry Profile and the Template for Industry Survey
2. Gather information on the industry.	
3. Analyze the industry. What can you conclude about the attractiveness of the industry over the next three years?	Strategy Session 6 – Forces Affecting Competitive Strategy
Phase II Two Competitors in Industry	
Identify two companies that are operating in the industry you have studied. Preferably, choose two that have had very different performances in the recent past. Divide the team into two subunits, and each unit will focus on one firm.	
1. Each team subunit should identify the current strategy of the firm and appraise its internal resources and capabilities. How is the current strategy incorporating these competencies and helping the firm compete within the industry?	Strategy Session 7 – Generating a Plan of Action: SWOT [TOWS] Analysis Strategy Session 8 – Developing Generic Strategy Strategy Session 9 – Building Competitive Advantage Strategy Session 10 – Viewing Corporate Strategy from the Core Competencies Perspective Session 17 – Strategy Implementation using the 7-S Model

2. Evaluate the current performance of the firm. How successful has the strategy been in generating an above-average financial performance of the firm over time and in relation to the industry and competitors? Template for Assessing Company Financial Performance

Phase III   Final Analysis

Reunite both subunits of the team and conduct the final analysis.

1. Compare the two firms. Faced with the same industry environment, examine how and why the firms pursued the strategies they did.

2. What are your recommendations for each of them? How would you change their strategies? What recommendations do you have for implementation?

Project B: Identifying Strategic Issues at Local Business Organizations

Phase I   Company Selection

Identify an organization in your local community. This must be a firm that you have access to both in terms of (1) being able to visit the offices and plants, and (2) being able to interview at least one company official. The company may be small or large and can operate either in the profit or nonprofit sector. If it is a large organization with divisions in several industries, such as General Electric, choose one of the divisions for this study.

Phase II Overview	Strategy Sessions/Industry Profile
Identify the industry in which the organization (or division) competes.	See Part IV – Lodging Industry Profile and the Template for Industry Survey
1. Gather information on the industry.	
2. Analyze the industry. What can you conclude about the attractiveness of the industry over the next three years?	Strategy Session 6 – Forces Affecting Competitive Strategy

Phase III Strategic Issues Identification	Strategy Sessions
1. Identify one or two major strategic issues the company faces. State them in a question form. To develop the issues, do *either* of the following:	
a. Develop a table of the definitions of strategy applied to the company. Analyze results from an intended versus emerged strategy perspective, which the definitions help to clarify.	Strategy Session 2 – Understanding the Concept of Strategy
b. Based on your reading of the firm and its environment, identify issues that you feel the company must tackle now in order to place it in a better position into the future.	Strategy Session 1 – Decision Making at the Strategic and Operational Level
2. After undertaking your analysis (including financial performance) based on publicly available information, meet with company officials and discuss your findings. Use their input to further refine your analysis. Bring your analysis to a conclusion with recommendations.	Strategy Session 7 – Generating a Plan of Action: SWOT [TOWS] Analysis OR Strategy Session 17 – Strategy Implementation using the 7-S Model

Report Format

Present your project work in the form of a written report and an oral presentation to the class. In the case of Project B, you may consider giving a copy of your report to the organization, or inviting the company official who was your contact to the class presentation. Your written report should:

1. Be no more than about 6,000 words (12 pages). Place all tables and charts in appendixes in the end.

2. Be organized in such a way that the report follows the phases of the project.

3. Include a complete list of references at the end of all published information, Web sites, and interviews that were sources of information.

Your presentation should last about 20 minutes. Do not repeat all the information in the report, but plan your presentation around the key points you wish to convey to the audience.

MICA
Method of Case Analysis and Discussion

The analysis of case studies is one of the most popular techniques for applying strategic management theory to real-life situations. Typically, you read a factual account of a problem or issue faced by an organization and then come to class prepared to discuss the situation and make recommendations.

The MICA method is an approach to case discussion that is designed to increase student preparation and bring about full-class participation. Its focus is on discussion of the case versus a formal presentation of the case by a team of students. There are four main components to the MICA process:

1. Students submit before class a proposed strategic-level and an operational-level action step (a recommended course of action that the company should take).
2. During the class, a student team administers the case discussion.
3. Class members discuss the action steps proposed by the class and vote on the most acceptable course of action.
4. The instructor evaluates the students based on what they say at the time they say it using established MICA scoring criteria.

For each case that is assigned, a team of students administers the case discussion. The remaining students submit action steps to this administrative team before the entire class meets to discuss the case.

Action Steps

Action steps are suggestions to improve the situation described in the case. Each student submits one proposed course of action that is strategic in nature and another that is operational or functional in scope (see Strategy Session 1). For example, a strategic action step might be to sell off one of the company's divisions or to change the company's generic strategy from differentiation to cost leadership. An operational or functional action step might be to develop a new advertising campaign or hire more people in the accounts payable department. The action steps do not include any justification for the proposed action; the students provide justification later during the class discussion.

Administrative Team

The administrative team collects action steps, compiles them, types a listing, and distributes them to the class either just before or during class. The action steps are grouped into two main categories: strategic and operational. The author's last name is shown at the end of each action step in parentheses. Because it is common for two or more students to submit similar action steps, there may be multiple authors for an action step. The team may list authors in the order in which the steps are received, determine the order of authors according to the completeness of the action step submitted, or list authors on a random basis.

The administrative team does not present or discuss the case but rather is responsible for *administering* class discussion. The team's roles include a chairperson, a counter, and as many recorders as needed. In small classes, teams may consist of as few as two persons (chairperson-recorder roles being combined and a counter) to as many as six (three students handle compiling and typing the action steps; the other three students conduct the case discussion as chairperson, counter, and recorder).

The counter keeps track of how many times each class member has been called on and assists the chairperson in selecting speakers. This process is designed to provide an equal discussion opportunity for those who wish to participate. The recorder puts on the board any action steps that were modified at the start of class. He or she lists all action steps being discussed and records the outcome of each action step.

Process

1. Introduction
The administrative team arrives early to class. Action steps are distributed to the other members of the class as they arrive. The team signals the start of class by introducing all members of the team, identifying the company to be discussed, and the time frame on which the discussion should center.

2. Modifications of Action Steps
To begin the case discussion, the chairperson asks if the team has compiled any modifications or amendments to the action steps. For example, a member of the class might suggest that Step 5, which is to sell the clothing division of the company, is similar to Step 12, which is to divest an operation. The administrative team consults with the authors of both steps and decides whether the steps should be combined.

3. Discussion of Strategic-level Step
Once the proposed action steps have been modified or clarified, the team begins discussion of strategic-level action steps by selecting the first action step from the list. Those from the class who authored the action step are called on first to provide their rationale for the proposed course of action. (Because the authors of a particular action step are called on first, they have the opportunity to present the strongest arguments, which is the basis for the scoring system.) Once the authors have completed their discussion, any class member who wishes to support or argue against the step raises his or her hand and is called on by the team chairperson. The administrative team is responsible for cutting off "long-winded" discussions and terminating discussions of a particular course of action when arguments become redundant.

After an action step has been thoroughly discussed, the administrative team conducts a vote of the class whether to accept or reject the action step. If accepted, it becomes a fact of the case. At this point, the administrative team randomly chooses three or four strategic-level action steps (usually from an envelope containing the numbers for each action step). Then the class votes on what step to discuss next. Class members may vote for more than one step; and the chairperson breaks any ties. This process continues until all strategic steps are discussed or until the administrative team feels it is time to move on to operational-level steps.

4. Operational-level Action Steps
The administrative team guides the discussion of operational-level courses of action in the same way that the strategic steps were handled. This continues until approximately 10 to 15 minutes before the class period ends. Typically, the majority of strategic-level action steps are discussed and three or four operational-level steps are covered.

5. Closing the Case Discussion
The administrative team ends the discussion of action steps 10 to 15 minutes before the class period ends. (Typically, there are operational-level action steps that are not discussed. However, students are reminded that the major emphasis of the course is on strategic decision making.) Then the chairperson asks the class if anyone prepared research that was not used during the class discussion ("unspent research"). One article

per class member is allowed, and students receive additional credit based on their oral summary of the article's content as it applies to a particular action step. These summaries are brief and take 1 to 2 minutes at most.

The administrative team delivers a brief summary of the decisions made by the class and asks its members to spend a few minutes thinking about their class discussion. Have they helped the company with their strategic decisions? Did they notice any pattern in the steps chosen or in the class's discussion? For example, during one session, every action step got a "no" vote. Several class members noted this was because the company had been losing money, and people were reluctant to make any major changes.

Scoring

The instructor, seated at the back of the room, assigns points to class members based on the content and frequency of their arguments. Each time a student speaks, he or she may earn from 0 to 4 points, plus bonus points judged by the instructor. Authors of action steps speak first and have the greatest opportunity to back up their argument with facts not yet given. This means, of course, that authors tend to accumulate points quickly. In addition, the first time any class member speaks, he or she is awarded one bonus point regardless of content to encourage participation and give evidence of attendance.

For each case, a student may earn a minimum of 0 and a maximum of 25 points. Students receive points only if their comment is relevant to the action step being discussed, if it contains a supportive argument, and if it is not a repeat of what was said by another student earlier in the discussion. The score for each member of the administrative team equals the highest points allocated to any student for that day; thus the team has an incentive to keep the discussion moving along so that fellow class members will score points.

When the last action step has been discussed and the vote recorded, the instructor asks if any class member feels that he or she was discriminated against (for example, consistently had a hand up but was not called on). If a student indicates that this occurred, the instructor asks the administrative team's counter (a) how many times the class member was called on in a nonauthor priority call; and (b) excluding author calls, what was the average number of times students were called on that day. The administrative team comments on the alleged discrimination, and the instructor considers his or her own observations and the statements of the student and the administrative team. If it is judged that discrimination occurred, the student is given one to three first discussion opportunities (after the authors) during the next case. In addition, 3 to 10 points may be deducted from the case grade of each member of the administrative team for that case. Under these circumstances, bona fide cases of discrimination rarely occur.

Scores are posted on a spreadsheet at the end of class, using student identification numbers for confidentiality.

Instructor's Roles

The instructor's roles include coaching, scoring, altering the course of debate during the case discussion as required, enforcing MICA rules as needed, and providing a wrap-up at the end of the period. The instructor may intervene at any time during the class for the purpose of guiding discussion or coaching students.

For example, the instructor may accept or reject an action step without allowing discussion if it is deemed a standard business practice or it is too trivial to be discussed given the context of the case. Suppose the class voted to discussion an action step such as "The company needs a mission statement." The instructor should stop the process, remind the class that this action step as it stands is a normally expected business practice, and indicate that it would be difficult to develop arguments against this step. The author should develop a proposed mission statement and submit it as an action step, which can then be debated.

Coaching is a way of showing students how to score points. It is used extensively in the first few cases or in a trial case. An example of coaching would be an intervention by the instructor after a student comment. The instructor would note that the student did not score points because someone else had already made the comment or that no points were scored because the research presented did not apply to the action step being discussed.

If necessary, altering the course of debate is important, particularly during the early cases. If the class discussion moves away from the specifics of the action step being discussed and if the administrative team does not quickly refocus the discussion, the instructor must interrupt immediately and note what has happened, reminding the class that no points are awarded for these digressions.

At the end of the period, the instructor asks the class members if, in their opinion, they have helped the company. Students comment on their perceptions, and as the semester progresses, they usually become more aware of the quality of their decisions. For example, one group discussed a company that had been a takeover target and had high levels of debt. Yet in the wrap-up session, the group noted that, although they considered the debt when discussing courses of action (difficult to get loans for expansion and the like), the final strategies they recommended did not help the company become more solvent. Several students noted that the class lost sight of the company's difficult debt situation and relied entirely on management's bright forecast for future sales and earnings.

The instructor can also use the end-of-session comments for a review of the case, update the case information, or highlight important issues that the students did not cover in their action steps. A few minutes highlighting the key points of the discussion gives students a sense of satisfaction that they hit the important issues, or insight into how a key learning of the case got missed in the discussion.

Summary

Student preparation for class discussion of cases is extensive. Since points are awarded based on information to support or rebut an action step, students read the cases very thoroughly. For example, it is not atypical for students to cite phrases from the case text, as well as information from tables and footnotes. Discussion is also lively. Since points are based primarily on how often students speak and what they say, class participation is very strong.

In addition, some preliminary evidence suggests that students using the MICA method reported better preparation and participation benefits as compared to students using other methods of case discussion. Also, students using the MICA method were better able to identify the main focus of the cases discussed, showing a better recall of content issues involved in case discussions.

REFERENCES AND SOURCES

Strategy Session 1 L. J. Bourgeois III, I. M., Duhaime, and J. L. Stimpert, *Strategic Management: A Managerial Perspective,* 2nd ed. (Forth Worth, TX: Dryden, 1999), 10–11; Michael E. Porter, What is strategy?, *Harvard Business Review* 74, no. 6 (1996), 61–78.

Strategy Session 2 Charles W. L. Hill and Gareth R. Jones, *Strategic Management: An Integrated Approach,* 8th ed. (Boston: Houghton Mifflin, 2008), 3; Michael A Hitt, R. Duane Ireland, and Robert Hoskisson, *Strategic Management: Competitiveness and Globalization Concepts and Cases,* 8th ed. (Cincinnati, OH: South-Western/Cengage, 2009), 5; Charles W. Hofer and Dan Schendel, *Strategy Formulation: Analytical Concepts* (St. Paul, MN: West, 1978), 4; Henry Mintzberg, Five Ps for strategy, *California Management Review* 30, no. 1 (1987), 11–25.

Strategy Session 3 Dereck E. Abell, *Defining the Business: The Starting Point of Strategic Planning.* (Englewood Cliffs, NJ: Prentice Hall, 1980); James C. Collins and Jerry I. Porras, Building your company's vision, *Harvard Business Review* 74, no. 5 (1996), 65–77; Jim Collins, It's not what you make, it's what you stand for, *Inc.* 19, no. 14 (1997), 42–45; Jerry Knapp, A mission statement, *Firehouse,* March 1992, 70–71; Lance Leuthesser and Chiranjeev Kohli, Corporate identity: The role of mission statements, *Business Horizons* 40, no. 3 (1997), 59–66. **Sources for exercise 1:** Harley-Davidson and Continental Airlines mission statements used with permission. Use of Medtronic mission courtesy of Medtronic, Inc.

Strategy Session 4 C. Gopinath, J. Siciliano, & R. Murray, Changing role of the board of directors: In search of a new strategic identity?, *Mid-Atlantic Journal of Business* 30, no. 2 (1994), 175–185; Why CEOs need to be honest with their boards, *Wall Street Journal,* January 14, 2008, R1–R3. **Sources for part I of the exercise:** R. L. Simison, GM board adopts formal guidelines on stronger control over management, *Wall Street Journal,* March 28, 1994, A4. *Note:* The authors thank General Motors for permission to use their guidelines. An abridged version of the May 2007 guidelines is provided for this exercise. **Sources for part II of the exercise:** Enron Corporation, *Annual report 2002*; Enron Corporation, *Report of Special Investigating Committee,* February 1, 2002; J. S. Lublin and J. R. Emshwiller, Enron Board's actions raise liability questions, *Wall Street Journal,* January 17, 2002.

Strategy Session 5 R. E. Freeman, *Strategic Management: A Stakeholder Approach* (Boston: Pitman, 1984), 25, 53–54; Charles W. L. Hill and T. M. Jones, Stakeholder-agency theory, *Journal of Management Studies* 29 (1992), 131–154. *Source for the Wal-Mart exercise:* Arthur E. Wilmarth, Jr., May 2008, Subprime crisis confirms wisdom of separating banking and commerce, *Banking & Financial Services Policy Report* 27, no. 5, 1–18; Kris Hudson and Rob Wells, Wal-Mart cancels its bank plan; Halt to ILC effort is move by retailer to stop controversy, *Wall Street Journal,* March 17, 2007, A3; Gary McWilliams, Woes mount for Wal-Mart in bank move, *Wall Street Journal,* January 19, 2007, A3.

Strategy Session 6 A. Brandenburger and B. Nalebuff, *Co-opetition* (New York: Doubleday, 1996); Michael E. Porter, How competitive forces shape strategy, *Harvard Business Review* 57, no. 2 (1979), 137–145; R. M. Grant, *Contemporary Strategy Analysis* (Oxford: Blackwell, 2002); Andrew S. Grove, Surviving a 10x force, *Strategy and Leadership* 25, no. 1 (1997), 35–38; Thomas L. Wheelen and J. David Hunger, *Strategic Management and Business Policy,* 11th ed. (Upper Saddle River, NJ: Prentice Hall, 2008).

Strategy Session 7 Kenneth R. Andrews, *The Concept of Corporate Strategy* (Homewood, IL: Irwin, 1980); Fred R. David, *Strategic Management Concepts,* 11th ed. (Upper Saddle River, NJ: Prentice Hall, 2007); Weihrich, The TOWS Matrix: A tool for situational analysis, *Long Range Planning* 15, no. 2 (1982), 54–66. **Source for Robin Hood:** Copyright © 1991 by Joseph Lampel, University of Nottingham, England. Reprinted with permission.

Strategy Session 8 Michael E. Porter, *Competitive Advantage* (New York: Free Press, 1985); Michael E. Porter, Toward a dynamic theory of strategy, *Strategic Management Journal* 12 (1991), 95–117; James F. Lincoln, *A New Approach to Industrial Economics* (New York: Devin-Adair, 1961), 126–127. **Source for exercise and team activity:** Adapted from Anisya Thomas, Introducing students to business policy and strategy: Two exercises to increase participation and interest, *Journal of Management Education* 23, no. 4 (1999), 428–437. Used with permission.

Strategy Session 9 C. Campbell-Hunt, What have we learned about generic competitive strategy? A meta analysis, *Strategic Management Journal,* 21, (2000), 127–154. G. Jones, Determined to differentiate, *Marketing,* October 31, 2007, 20; S. Kotha and B.L. Vadlamani, Assessing generic strategies: An empirical investigation of two competing typologies in discrete manufacturing industries, *Strategic Management Journal* 16, (1995), 75–83. Henry Mintzberg, Generic strategies: Toward a comprehensive framework, *Advances in Strategic Management,* no. 5 (1988), 1–67.

Strategy Session 10 J. B. Barney, Firm resources and sustained competitive advantage, *Journal of Management* 17 (1991), 99–120; J. B. Barney, Looking inside for competitive advantage, *Academy of Management Executive* 9, no. 4 (1995), 56; R. M. Grant. The resource-based theory of competitive advantage: Implications for strategy formulation, *California Management Review* 33 (1991), 114–135; G. Hamel and C. K. Prahalad, *Competing for the Future* (Cambridge, MA: Harvard Business School, 1994), 227. **Sources for Honda profile:** Alex Taylor III, Inside Honda's brain, *Fortune* 157, no. 5 (March 17, 2008), 100–106; Honda Annual Report 2008; Honda Motor Company Limited, November 19, 2007, *DataMonitor.* Published in www.datamonitor.com.—relocate reference per comment.

Strategy Session 11 P. A. Sudarsanam, *The Essence of Mergers and Acquisitions* (London: Prentice Hall, 1995); M. Y. Yoshino and U. S. Rangan, *Strategic Alliances* (Boston: Harvard Business School, 1995). *Sources for NUMMI: The General Motors–Toyota Alliance exercise:* Donald W. Nauss, GM, Toyota team up to develop technologies, *Los Angeles Times,* April 20, 1999, C1; Lindsay Chappell, Chief of Toyota pickup plant got his schooling at GM, *San Diego Union-Tribune,* September 19, 1998, C4; Michael Macoby, Farewell to the factory: Auto workers in the late twentieth century, *Harvard Business Review* 75, no. 6 (1997), 161–168; Clair Brown and Michael Reich, When does union-management cooperation work?: A look at NUMMI and GM-Van Nuys, *California Management Review* 31, no. 4 (1989), 26–44; Automakers eye US corporate citizenship, *Nikkei Weekly,* July 22, 2003; A. Inkpen, Learning through alliances: General Motors and NUMMI, *California Management Review* 47, no. 4 (2005); A. Chozick and N. Shirouzu, GM slips into Toyota's rearview mirror, *Wall Street Journal,* April 25, 2007, A7; N. Shirozou, Toyota's new US plan: Stop building factories, *Wall Street Journal,* June 20, 2007, A14; A. Morse, Toyota's problem with Japan, *Wall Street Journal,* February 7, 2007, A9.

Strategy Session 12 C. A. Bartlett, S. Ghoshal & P. Beamish, *Transnational Management* (Boston: McGraw-Hill/Irwin, 2008); Yoo Soh-jung, Korea essential to Pernod Ricard's growth strategy, *The Korea Herald*, April 24, 2006. *Sources for Bata Shoe Organization profile in exercise:* Bata Limited, About us, http://www.bata.com/main.html (2008); Betty J. Punnett, Bata Shoe Organization, in *Experiencing International Business and Management*, 2nd ed. (Belmont, CA: Wadsworth, 1994), 127–128; Bernard Simon, Bata in transition, *Financial Times Limited,* June 6 (1996), 28; C.R. Sukumar, Bata may cut staff to keep its sole tight, *Business Line,* June 18, 2003; Uganda: High costs force firms to relocate, *Africa News*, February 27, 2007; Marina Strauss, Athletes World deal falters, *The Globe and Mail*, November 5, 2007, B1. *Sources for Nike, Inc. profile in exercise:* Nike, Inc., http://www.nikebiz.com (2008); M. Jill Austin, Nike-2004, in *Cases in Strategic Management*, Fred R. David, ed. (Upper Saddle River, NJ: Pearson Prentice Hall, 2005), 495–511; Louise Lee, Can Nike still do it?, *Business Week*, February 21, 2000, 120–128; Maureen Tkacik, As extreme goes mass, Nike nips are skate-show icon, *Wall Street Journal*, April 24, 2002, A1; On the run, *Forbes*, February 11, 2008, 83–87.

Strategy Session 13 C. Gopinath, Turnaround: Recognizing decline and initiating intervention, *Long Range Planning* 24, no. 6 (1991), 96–101; Charles. W. Hofer, Turnaround strategies, *Journal of Business Strategy* 1 (1980), 19–31; D. K. Robbins and John A. Pearce, Turnaround: retrenchment and recovery, *Strategic Management Journal* 13 (1992), 287–309.

Strategy Session 14 Arie De Geus, *The Living Company* (Boston: Harvard Business School, 1997); Peter Schwartz, *The Art of the Long View* (New York: Doubleday, 1991); Ian Wylie, There is no alternative to . . . TINA, *Fast Company* 60 (July 2002); Bernard Wysocki, Jr., Soft landing or hard? Firm tests strategy on 3 views of future, *Wall Street Journal*, July 7, 2000, A1; Bob Davis, Rise of nationalism frays global ties, *Wall Street Journal*, April 28, 2008, A1; G. Burt et al., The role of scenario planning in exploring the environment in vies of the limitations of PEST and its derivatives, *International Studies of Management & Organization*, 36 (2006), 50–76.

Strategy Session 15 Kenneth R. Andrews, *The Concept of Corporate Strategy* (Homewood, IL: Dow Jones Irwin, 1971); Henry Mintzberg, Patterns in strategy formulation, *Management Science* 24 (1978), 934–948; R. A. Burgelman and A. S. Grove, Strategic dissonance, *California Management Review* 38, no. 2 (1996), 8–28; Thomas V. Bonoma, *The Marketing Edge: Making Strategies Work* (New York: Free Press, 1985), 10–14; Cornelis A. DeKluyver, *Strategic Thinking: An Executive Perspective* (Upper Saddle River, NJ: Prentice Hall, 2000), 56–57. *Sources for Hewlett-Packard exercise:* Quentin Hardy, The unCarly, *Forbes* 179, no. 5 (March 12, 2007), 82–90; Ben Elgin, The inside story of Carly's ouster, *Business Week* 3921 (February 21, 2005), 34–35; Memo to Mark Hurd, *Business Week* 3928 (April 11, 2005), 38–39.

Strategy Session 16 Alfred D. Chandler, *Strategy and Structure* (Cambridge, MA: MIT, 1962); Joseph A. Litterer, *Organizations: Structure and Behavior*, 3rd ed. (New York: Wiley, 1980); J. R. Galbraith and R. K. Kazanjian, *Strategy Implementation: The Role of Structure and Process,* 2nd ed. (St. Paul, MN: West, 1986). *Source for exercise:* Adapted from Cheryl Harvey and Kim Morouney, Organizational structure and design: The Club Ed exercise, *Journal of Management Education* 22, no. 3 (1998), 425–430. Used with permission.

Strategy Session 17 R. H. Waterman, Thomas J. Peters, and J. R. Phillips, Structure is not an organization, *Business Horizons* (June 1980), 14–26; Dexter Dunphy and Doug Stace, The strategic management of corporate change, *Human Relations* 46 (1993), 905–920. *Sources for PeopleSoft case in exercise:* George Avalos, Pleasanton, Calif.-based software firm workers welcome new president, *Contra Costa Times*, May 25, 1999; David Bank, Despite assurance, PeopleSoft to cut jobs, *Wall Street Journal,* September 4, 2003, B4; PeopleSoft names Craig A. Conway as chief executive officer, *Business Wire, Inc.*, September 21, 1999; Jessica Guynn, Pleasanton, Calif.-based PeopleSoft invites workers' parents for a day, *Contra Costa Times*, August 7, 1998; Jessica Guynn, Executive describes pain at California-based PeopleSoft after layoffs, *Contra Costa Times*, January 30, 1999; Quentin Hardy, A software star sees its "family" culture turn dysfunctional, *Wall Street Journal,* May 5, 1999, A1; Carleen Hawn, Now for my next trick, *Forbes*, January 21, 2002,

90–92; David Whelan, PeopleSoft merger to blend differing business philosophies, *Contra Costa Times,* June 3, 2003; Bryce G. Hoffman, Calif.-based PeopleSoft reclaims place as software leader, *Contra Costa Times*, September 19, 1999. Jessica Twentyman, Joined up thinking, *Personnel Today*, April 25, 2006, 25–27; Cheryl Meyer, Culture Shock, *The Deal.com*, September 22, 2003; Cheryl Meyer, Pyrrhic Victory, *The Deal.com*, September 8, 2006.

Strategy Session 18 Milton Friedman, The social responsibility of business is to increase its profits, *New York Times Magazine*, September 13, 1970, 33, 122–126; Neil Jacoby, *Corporate Power and Social Responsibility* (New York: Macmillan, 1973), 6; Frederick D. Sturdivant and Heidi Vernon-Wortzel, *Business and Society: A Managerial Approach*, 4th ed. (Homewood, IL: Irwin, 1990).

Strategy Session 19 Daniel Covell, Sharianne Walker, Julie Siciliano, and Peter Hess, *Managing Sports Organizations*, 2nd ed. (Orlando, FL: Elsevier, Inc., 2007), 166–167; Robert Kaplan and David Norton, The balanced scorecard: Measures that drive performance, *Harvard Business* Review 70, no. 1 (1992), 71–79; Robert Kaplan and David Norton, Using the balanced scorecard as a strategic management system, *Harvard Business Review* 74, no. 1 (1996), 75–85; Gopal Kanji and Patricia Moura e Sa, Kanji's Business Scorecard, *Total Quality Management* 13, no. 1 (2002), 13–27.

Part IV *Sources for Lodging Industry profile:* Mark Basham, Standard & Poor's, *Industry Surveys*, Lodging & Gaming, May 22, 2008; Robert Mandelbaum, In hindsight 2007 looks great, *Hotel News Resource*, August 20, 2008, http://www.hotelnewsresoure.com; Robert Mandelbaum and Steven Nicholas, Select financial performance, *Hotel News Resource,* June 23, 2008; Bureau of Labor Statistics, U.S. Department of Labor, *Career Guide to Industries, 2008–09 Edition,* Hotels and Other Accommodations, http://www.bls.gov/oco/eg/egs036.htm; Jan Freitag, Industry's momentum can be traced to construction, *Hotel & Motel Management*, 28, June 2, 2008.

Source for Mercury Telecom case: Case prepared by Prof. Stephen Courter, McCombs School of Business, University of Texas at Austin, Austin, Texas, U.S., as a basis for class discussion and not to represent effective or ineffective management. The case describes a real situation with suitable changes to maintain confidentiality. We thank him for his contribution.

Sources for Caffeine Satisfaction case: Steve Adams, Dunkin' Donuts CEO tweaking recipe for profits, *Patriot Ledger*, August 16, 2003, 36; Faith Arner, Can Dunkin' KO Krispy?, *Business Week* Online, July 3, 2003; E. M. Bossong-Martines (ed.), Standard & Poor's *Industry Surveys*, Foods & Nonalchoholic Beverages (New York: McGraw Hill, 2003); James Collins, A hot cup of Giuseppe, *Boston Globe*, September 2, 2003, E1; Bella English, Dunkin' Doughnuts setting off a war of glazed proportions, *Boston Globe*, June 24, 2003, E1; Bill Galatis, CEO of Watermark Donut Co., interview with authors, November 26, 2003; Tina Grant (ed.), Allied Domecq PLC, *International Directory of Company Histories,* vol. 29 (St. James Press, Detroit, 2000); Dunkin Donuts (E): 1988 Distribution strategies, Case # 9-589-01, *Harvard Business Publishing* (2000); Howard Schultz and Starbucks Coffee Company, Case # 9-801-361, *Harvard Business School Publishing* (2001); Mark Maremont, Krispy Kreme sales seem to show signs of a sugar crash, *Wall Street Journal*, September 16, 2003, C1; J. P. Pedersen (ed.), Starbucks Corporation, *International Directory of Company Histories*, vol. 34 (St. James Press, Detroit, 2000); Ethical coffee pushed into mainstream, *Business Line*, July 3, 2003, 11; For Starbucks, there's no place like home, *Business Week,* June 9, 2003, 48; Starbucks' Howard Schultz, on America's caffeine fix, *Boston Globe*, April 18, 2004, C1; Janet Adamy, Dunkin' Donuts tries to go upscale but not too far, *Wall Street Journal*, April 8–9, 2006, A1; Janet Adamy, Starbucks chairman says trouble may be brewing, *Wall Street Journal*, February 24–25, 2007, A4.

Part V *Sources for MICA Method of Case Discussion:* Ramarao Desiraju and C. Gopinath, Encouraging participation in case discussions: A comparison of the MICA and the Harvard case methods, *Journal of Management Education* 25, no. 4 (2001), 394–408; Julie Siciliano and Gordon M. McAleer, Increasing student participation in case discussions: Using the MICA method in strategic management courses, *Journal of Management Education* 21, no. 2 (1997), 209–220.

INDEX

A

Abbott Laboratories, 22
Accor S. A., 136
Activity ratios, 141–142
Andarr, P. L., 37
Andrews, Kenneth R., 47
Arthur D. Little matrix, 65
AT&T, 13

B

Bafunno, Norm, 74, 75
Balanced scorecard, 127–131
Banking services, Wal-Mart strategy and, 30–31
Bankruptcy, 88
Bargaining power
    of buyers, 38
    of suppliers, 37
Barriers to entry, 37
Bata Shoe Organization (BSO), 81–82
BCG growth/share matrix, 65
Bear Stearns, 30
Belfer, Robert A., 27
Ben & Jerry's, 121
Best-cost position, 56
Best Western International, 136
Blake, Norman P., 27
Bleeke, Joel, 71
Board of directors
    Enron, 26–28
    General Motors, 23–26
    guidelines for, 23–26
    role of, in corporate governance, 21–28
Boundary spanner, 21
Boyd Gaming, 40
BP, 124–125
Broad market scope, 55
Business processes, 127
Buyers, bargaining power of, 38

C

Canon, 66
Capellas, Michael, 103
Caribou Coffee, 18, 157
Case studies
    coffee retailing industry, 149–157
    Mercury Telecom, 143–148
    MICA method of analysis and discussion, 163–166
Casino gambling industry, 39–45
Chan, Ronnie C., 27
Chandler, Alfred, 107

Chapter 7 bankruptcy, 88
Chapter 11 bankruptcy, 88
Chief executive officer (CEO)
    relationship between board of directors and, 22
    role of, 21, 107
China, 41
Choice Hotels International, 136
Classical economics, 121
Coffee retailing industry, 149–157
Colorado Rockies, 129–131
Community, 29
Compaq, 103
Competition
    in casino gambling industry, 39–45
    industry, 37
Competition
    in lodging industry, 135–136
Competitive advantage
    building, 61–64
    core competencies and, 65–66
    generic strategy and, 55
    strategic-level decisions and, 4
Competitive scope, 55
Competitive strategy, forces affecting, 37–45
Complementors, 38
Continental Airlines, 14–15
Conway, Craig, 116–117
Core competencies perspective, 65–69
Core purpose, communicating, through mission
    statements, 11–19
Corporate governance
    board's role in, 21–28
    exercises, 23–28
    guidelines for, 22, 23–26
Corporate social responsibility, 121
Corporate strategy
    core competencies perspective on, 65–69
    at Honda, 67–69
    structure and, 107–112
Corporate sustainability, 121–125
Cost leadership, 55, 61
Creditors, 29
Credos, 13
Customers, 29, 127

D

Decision making
    operational-level, 3–4, 12–13
    strategic-level, 3–4
Decline, 87–91
Dell, 71

Design differentiation, 62
Differentiation, 55, 56
  design, 62
  image, 61
  price, 61
  quality, 62
  support, 61
Differentiation strategy, 55, 61–64
Downsizing, 65
Drucker, Peter F., 11, 21, 65, 121
Duffield, David A., 115–116, 117
Duke Energy Corporation, 93
Duncan, John H., 27
Dunkin' Donuts, 151–154

E

Emergent strategies, 101
Employees, 29
Enron Corporation, 22, 26–28
Entry barriers, 37
Environment, corporate sustainability and, 122
Equal Exchange, 149
Ernst, David, 71

F

Fair Trade Coffee, 149
Federal Reserve Board, 30–31
Financial analysis, 141–142
Financial perspective, 128
Fiorina, Carly, 103–104
Five P's, 7–8
Focus cost leadership, 55
Focus differentiation, 55
Focus-market scope, 56
Formulation, strategy, 101–102
Fossil, Inc., 19, 60
Franklin, Benjamin, 87
Freeman, R. Edward, 29, 122
Friedman, Milton, 121
Full-service hotels, 135–136
Functional structure, 107, 108

G

Galaxy Entertainment Group, 41
Game theory, 71
GE/McKinsey model, 65
General Electric (GE), 66
General Motors (GM), 22
  alliance between Toyota and, 73–78
  board guidelines, 23–26
Generic strategy
  competitive advantage and, 61–62
  developing, 55–60
  Fossil, Inc., 60
  team activity, 59
Globalization, 79
Global strategic alliances, 71–78
Global strategy, 79, 80
Goodyear Tire & Rubber Co., 22
Gore, Al, 122
Governance. *See* Corporate governance
Gramm, Wendy L., 27
Greyhound Lines, 22
Growth, 65

H

Harley-Davidson, 14–15
Harrah's Entertainment, 40, 41

Hewlett-Packard
  corporate sustainability, 122
  problem diagnosis at, 103–105
  strategic alliances, 71
Hilton Hotels, 136
Honda Motor Company, corporate strategy, 67–69
Hotel industry. *See* Lodging industry
Human resources, 128
Hurd, Mark, 104

I

IBM, 22
IKEA, 62
Image differentiation, 61
Implementation. *See* Strategy implementation
An Inconvenient Truth (film), 122
Industrial Loan Company (ILC), 30–31
Industry
  competition within, 37–38
  defined, 37
Industry competition, 37
Industry profile
  lodging industry, 135–138
Industry survey
  template for, 139–140
Innkeepers of America (exercise), 5–6
Institutional theory, 21–22
Intel, 71
InterContinental Hotels Group, 136
International Coffee Organization (ICO), 149
International Game Technology (IGT), 41
Internet gambling, 40–41

J

Jaedicke, Robert K., 27
Japan, 30
John Deere, 123
Johnson & Johnson, 13

K

Kelvin, Lord, 127
Kmart, 22
Krispy Kreme Doughnuts, 157
Kropf Fruit Company, 53–54

L

Lay, Kenneth, 27
Lean manufacturing, 75
Lemaistre, Charles A., 27
Leverage ratios, 141
Limited-service hotels, 136
Lincoln, James F., 55
Liquidity ratios, 142
Little, Arthur D., 65
Lodging industry
  average room rates, 136
  competitors, 135–136
  industry profile, 135–138
  overview, 135
  segments, 137–138
Lodging industry, generic strategy for, 57–58
Low-cost strategy, 55, 56

M

Macau, China, 41
Market segmentation
  in lodging industry, 137–138
Marriott International, 136

Management, turnaround, 87–91
Matrix design structure, 108–109
Maytag, 55
McDonald's, 157
McKinsey & Company, 113
Medtronic, Inc., 14–15
Mendelsohn, John, 27
Mercury Telecommunications (case study), 143–148
Mexico, 30
MICA method, 163–166
Microsoft, 71
Mintzberg, Henry, 7, 61
Mission statements, 11–19
    charting strategic course in, 12
    Colorado Rockies, 129–131
    creating (exercises), 18–19
    criteria for, 11
    defining organization's core purpose in, 11–12
    operational-level decisions and, 12–13
    philosophy and values in, 13
    sample, 14–15
    team activity, 16–17
Morley, Andrew, 61
Motorola, 12
Multidivisional structure, 107
Multidomestic strategy, 79, 80

N

National Indian Gaming Commission, 40
Native American Gaming Regulatory Act, 40
Network-type structure, 108
New entrants, threat of, 37
New United Motor Manufacturing Incorporated (NUMMI), 73–78
Niche market, 55
Nike Inc., 82–83
Nonstructure, 108

O

Okuda, Hiroshi, 74
Operational-level decisions, 3–4
    exercise, 5–6
    mission statements and, 12–13
Operational perspective, 3
Opportunities, 47
Organizational structure, 107–112
Our Common Future, 122

P

Pattern, strategy as a, 7, 8
Peet's Coffee & Tea Inc., 157
PeopleSoft, 115–119
PepsiCo, 123
Pereora, Paulo V. Ferraz, 28
Performance measures, 127–131
Perspective, strategy as a, 7, 8
Philosophy, 13
Plan, strategy as a, 7, 8
Ploy, strategy as a, 7–8
Porter, Michael E., 3, 37, 55–56
"Portfolio of business" approach, 65
Position, strategy as a, 7, 8
Powers, William C., 28
Price differentiation, 61
Pringuet, Pierre, 79
Problem diagnosis, 101–105
Profit ratios, 141
Products, substitute, 38

Public Accounting Oversight Board, 22
Purpose, communicating, through mission statements, 11–19

Q

Quality differentiation, 62

R

Royal Dutch/Shell group, 93–94

S

Sarbanes-Oxley Act, 22
Savage, Frank, 28
Scenario planning, 93–98
Schwartz, Peter, 93
Segmentation, 62
Services, substitute, 38
7-S Model, 113–119
Shimada, Haruo, 75
South Korea, 30
Stakeholders
    perspective of, on strategy, 29–34
    relative power of other, 38
    team activity, 34
    types of, 29
Stakeholder theory, 122
Starbucks, 29, 154–157
Starwood Hotels & Resorts, 136
Stockholders, 29
Strategic alliances
    defined, 71
    global, 71–78
Strategic business units (SBUs), 108
Strategic course, in mission statements, 12
Strategic-level decisions, 3–4
    exercise, 5–6
    scenario planning for, 93–98
Strategic management, sustainability and, 122–123
Strategic performance, assessment of, 141–142
Strategic thought process, 3, 4
Strategy
    core competencies perspective on, 65–69
    definitions of, 7–10
    emergent, 101
    generic, 55–60
    global, 79, 80
    multidomestic, 79, 80
    organizational structure and, 107–112
    as a pattern, 7, 8
    as a perspective, 7, 8
    as a plan, 7, 8
    as a ploy, 7–8
    as a position, 7, 8
    stakeholder perspective on, 29–34
    transnational, 79–85
Strategy formulation, 101–102
Strategy implementation, 101–102
    balanced scorecard and, 127–131
    using 7-S Model, 113–119
Strengths, 47
Structure, organizational, 107–112
Substitute products and services, 38
Sullivan, Louis H., 107
Suppliers
    bargaining power of, 37
    as stakeholders, 29
Support differentiation, 61
Sustainability, 121–125
SWOT analysis, 47–54

T

Team activities
  mission statement revision, 16–17
  negotiations, 77–78
  organizational structures, 110–112
  stakeholder group, 34
  top management team, 59
Team projects, 161–162
Threats, 47
Tim Hortons, 157
TOWS matrix, 47–54
Toyota, alliance between GM and, 73–78
Transaction cost analysis, 71, 72
Transnational strategies, 79–85
Troubh, Raymond, 28
Turnaround management, 87–91
Tyco, 22

U

Undifferentiation, 62
UN Global Compact, 123

Unlawful Internet Gaming Enforcement Act (UIGEA), 40
Utz Kapeh Foundation, 149

V

Values, 13
Villiers, Phillipe Auguste, 101
Virtual organization, 108

W

Wakeham, John, 28
Wal-Mart
  banking strategy, 30–31
  best-cost position, 56
Waterman, Robert H., Jr., 113
Weaknesses, 47
Weihrich, H., 47
Winokur, Herbert S., Jr., 28
WorldCom, 22
Wyndham Worldwide Corporation, 136

Z

Zenith, 12